T0275381

Introduction to
Russian–
English
Translation

Introduction to
Russian–
English
Translation

Tactics and Techniques
for the Translator

NATALIA STRELKOVA

Hippocrene Books, Inc.
New York

For information, address:
HIPPOCRENE BOOKS, INC.
171 Madison Avenue
New York, NY 10016
www.hippocrenebooks.com

Library of Congress Cataloging in Publication Data

Strelkova, Natalia.
  Introduction to Russian-English translation : tactics and techniques for
the translator / Natalia Strelkova.
    pages ; cm
  Includes bibliographical references.
  ISBN 978-0-7818-1267-2 (paperback)
  ISBN 0-7818-1267-4 (paperback)
  1. Russian language—Translating into English. 2. Translating and
interpreting. I. Title.
  PG2498.S77 2012
  491.78'02—dc23

                                                    2012001582

Printed in the United States of America

Acknowledgments

This author is grateful for the encouragement and valuable advice she has received from Lynn Visson, Sergei Chulaki, and Ivan Chulaki. And, of course, is grateful to all the Hippocrene editors involved in the long process of preparing for publication.

Contents

Preface:
Is this book for you?

In today's world, Russian is playing an increasingly important role. Since perestroika, even before the breakup of the Soviet Union, there has been a boom in Russian-American relations – political, business, scientific, social, and cultural (to say nothing of today's blogs and tweets). Diplomatic agreements, business and legal contracts, scientific and medical research papers, news and commentary, fiction, non-fiction, and reviews all require translation. While the flood of Russian émigrés to the U.S. has provided a wealth of Russian speakers, that does not mean that a native speaker of Russian – particularly one with no training in translation – can successfully render a text into a non-native language, namely English. And though there is now access to dozens of excellent new dictionaries, general and specialized, as well as online sources, and while Russian is taught in dozens of high schools and hundreds of colleges and universities, courses geared specifically to translation are few and far between. Exchange programs that send students to Russia for several months are beneficial for improving knowledge of the language, but they do not train translators. There is a very real need now for translators with an excellent knowledge of both Russian and English, as well as for teachers of translation who could provide professional guidance and practice.

The present book came into being gradually, over some thirty years. Not a textbook in the usual sense, it is intended as one translator's informal guide to the fascinating possibilities of our profession, including some previously overlooked. In addition to the traditional areas usually covered in the classroom, there is a conscious emphasis on translating journalistic idiom and the conversational Russian of everyday life. But no textbook can ever replace a solid grounding in the two languages and cultures with which the translator is working, as well as constant exposure to the literature, both classical and modern, the media (print, audio, video, TV, online), and live discourse in those languages.

The method used in compiling this book was mostly empirical. Dozens of examples from the day-to-day work of teaching, writing, translating, and editing furnished the material it contains. Translation theory, however, and socio-linguistics, as well as the experience of translating into both English and Russian have made us all increasingly aware of the complex issues involved in our efforts to provide more than a fuzzy reflection of what the author of the original meant to say. It is our hope that *Introduction to Russian-English Translation* will prove useful to the practicing as well as the aspiring translator, and that it may help to fill a gap in this field, which in the U.S. remains largely unexplored.

Introduction:
The Art of Translation

Is translation an art or a craft? Why do some insist that translation is an art, when all too often it results in a text that is simply hard to read? Ideally, the translator is like a talented artist who when he looks at his sitter or a landscape, sees something more than the ordinary viewer — he sees the essence of what is in front of him. A good translator has processed the textual information to allow the reader to see what he sees and feel what he is feeling. He acts as an invisible bridge between the author and the reader. That is what makes translation an art.

On the other hand, mastery of the craft is important, too, for an inept, ineffectual translator or interpreter can wreak havoc on any effort at communication. One quip featuring such a bungler once went the rounds in Moscow:

"You stole my purse!"
"Она говорит, вы у нее украли сумку."

"Здрасьте! Я ваша тетя!"
"She says to say hello and by the way, she is your aunt."

What led to this disastrous result is that the colloquial expression that actually means "*What? Are you crazy? / You can't be serious!*" was translated literally, word for word.

Other blunders, almost as laughable, happen when a translator does not cast a critical eye over his own translation. Otherwise, how could he let a phrase like the following get by: "*liquidate a fire*" for ликвидировать пожар? Or even "*liquidate flood damage*" for ликвидировать последствия наводнения? It is no excuse that a Russian look-alike (cognate) happens to have the same root as the English verb but is routinely used in the general semantic area of "*eliminate*," as in "*put out a fire*," or else implies that meaning, as in "*repair /deal with flood damage*."

The noble ideal of communication is often bogged down in difficulties, but the precise nature of translation problems can be hard to pin down. Sometimes it seems as though our English doesn't make sense, or doesn't sound right. This book is an attempt to resolve such problems when translating from Russian into

English and to call attention to clues in the original that can help cope with them

The translator must be able to recognize pitfalls in the original Russian that might throw his English rendering off course. Russian words, phrases, and sentences need to be "decoded" and reformulated in English. Otherwise, the result may be a misinterpretation of the original thought, or even general confusion. If each individual Russian word and the original word order are blithely carried over into the translation, the reader is in for a jerky ride. How long he chooses to subject himself to such a strain depends on how much time he has and how badly he needs to know the content of the original! The translator's work is governed by the imperative need to put key words in key locations in the English sentence—and these may differ radically from the Russian original. Recognizing that fundamental difference between Russian and English syntax is critical to translation. To do a proper job the translator must first identify the key words in the Russian sentence, then build the English sentence around them.

Syntax plays a particularly crucial role in our work. Whether you are an aspiring or an experienced (but frustrated!) translator, you will feel liberated once you know the numerous ways to get around difficulties—and "getting around" them is no sin. Some tactics involve grammatical manipulation: changing the part of speech, moving a word or phrase to a different place in the sentence, breaking up or consolidating sentences, and occasionally doing a major makeover to get the author's idea across. Then there are special translator's maneuvers that approach the content from a different angle, while preserving the author's idea intact. Above all, attention should focus on locating and highlighting the main points in the sentence or paragraph and avoiding distraction by secondary elements.

Paradoxically, the translation of individual words is not always so important. What is needed is to convey the author's ideas—not necessarily his words—in the target language. Imagine the situation the author is describing, and try to find the appropriate phrases and idioms to communicate that in English. Before starting out, read through the entire Russian text, or as much of it as feasible. Break down each sentence into sense units and test out several ways to handle each one, then the whole sentence, paraphrasing where necessary. A word-for-word translation could turn out to be a complete misinterpretation, and get the perpetrator into serious trouble besides. Or at best, produce a comic effect he did not bargain for. One example:

"Тоже мне знаток нашелся!"

Not recognizing the heavy sarcasm in the original, one "creative" translator came up with this solution to an expression unfamiliar to him:

"I've found that I'm a connoisseur now, too!"

An acceptable translation would read something like:

"Since when have you been such an expert?"
"Some connoisseur, I must say!"

And finally, remember that one and the same word can have different meanings in different circumstances. We all know that **да** and **нет** are diametrical opposites. But is that always true? Look at the two of them when used in the same sentence:

"Да нет, говорю тебе, никогда не пойду на такое!"

Here, strangely enough, the **да** is used to accentuate the **нет**.
A possible translation:

"I've already told you, I'll never agree to a thing like that."

Or if **да** and **нет** appear together but in reverse order, that will signify insistence on an earlier statement in the <u>affirmative</u>:

"Нет, да. Сказала я, что пойду за него и вот — пойду!"
"I said I would. I <u>am</u> going to marry him, and that's that!"

Or in a different scenario, but with the same emphasis and some of the same words:

"Нет, да! Пойду я с тобой и все тут! "
"Oh, yes I will! I'm going with you, definitely!"

The best way to convey the author's idea may be far removed from a literal rendering of words, phrases, and syntax.

Even when dealing with texts such as legal or technical documents that require that each and every word be reflected, the translator should try to convey the meaning, if not necessarily the form of the original. This entails navigating between accuracy and readability while remaining true to the substance and tone of the original.

Of course, Russian and English differ enormously, starting with the alphabet, and including word formation and all aspects of grammar. Russian is highly inflected and contains all sorts of affixes. Then there are the dissimilarities in syntax and styles, including the sharp divide in Russian between formal and informal presentation (this book explores both). Yet the two languages have much in common. Both are rich in variety and nuance. Both make extensive use of historical allusion and modern coinages. The important and immensely rewarding job of the translator is to:

1. Delve into and decode the meaning of the original, often hidden under layers of lexical and syntactic complexity

2. Find ways to reformulate the sense and tone of the Russian in clear, forceful and elegant English

It may seem counterintuitive to state that the words of the original text are irrelevant. Yet if you translate each one individually, that may prove to be the case. Only if these words are taken together and understood as a single unit that makes up a thought can that thought be restated in the language of translation, the target language. And that's where your intuition as a native speaker of English comes into play.

No division into sections—accurate, readable, correct—can be airtight or waterproof. Language contains multiple interacting components and a translator has many potential solutions to choose from. Sometimes, however, such a menu of choices is not immediately obvious if a problem itself is not recognized as such. For this reason, it may be advisable to work through each category separately, but then allow the information contained in each to percolate until it settles into an integrated "data bank," accessible when needed.

The examples and texts in this book show what we face when attempting to set up a reliable system of communication between people of different cultures in which language plays such a vital part. Linguistic danger signals are flagged and illustrated by some infelicitous translations and suggested improvements. Those "not-so-good" translations, provided here as examples to be avoided, are sometimes misleading, but for the most part, they are too literal, too awkward, or just plain tedious. With little or no knowledge of Russian life, traditions, or written style, the average English-language reader is occasionally forced to guess at the Russian author's meaning and the beliefs and values underlying the text. This culture gap grows wider when key words and logical accents are misplaced in the translation. Pragmatic adjustments designed to assist the reader are part and parcel of the translator's job—if the translator is truly willing to be the bridge that enables communication.

If the procedures that follow seem to involve too much work for the translator in a hurry, remember that our ideas are not intended as immediate solutions meant for someone rushing to meet a deadline. They merely point out different facets of a translator's thinking.

Some translators can arrive at solutions empirically, "do-it-yourself" fashion, through a combination of practice, intuition, and luck. For those few lucky souls the answer appears spontaneously, as words and syntax flash through the brain, ready for instant use. But typically, the ability to always come up with a good translation takes years of experience and training, and even mature professionals can benefit from each other's experience.

CHAPTER 1

PRINCIPAL AIMS OF TRANSLATION

Translations must be:

Accurate. That means clarity in conveying the intention of the author as you understand it after reaching for the meaning behind the words. Such in-depth comprehension requires a firm grasp of Russian grammar and usage, as well as a feel for the right dictionary equivalent of the individual word, including denotation and connotation in the specific context. Accurate interpretation of the specific text involves detecting subtle differences in the degree of emphasis, lexical and syntactic, in order to get the author's idea across without being hypnotized by each individual word.

Correct. Employing good English grammar and stylistically and culturally appropriate usage is critical so that the register in English suits the relevant genre, fits in with the context, and meets the reader's expectations. In so doing, the translator can faithfully convey the image the author wishes to create.

Readable. Unfortunately, translated literature, both factual and fictional, is often hard to read. Texts in translation are frequently clumsy when the original reads smoothly, or flat when the original is colorful. They may seem bombastic or oddly overstated. For the Russian reader, who can connect the dots in his native language, the intended meaning of the original will come through anyway, but a translator who adheres too closely to the Russian form faces the ever-present problem of inappropriate usage in English, especially when making use of collocations in which the author's idea can literally get "lost in the translation."

The following pages demonstrate options (word choice and syntax) that the translator should consider in order to provide an easier read. They show what changes can be made to aid comprehension (pragmatic additions) and which ones would help produce the desired effect (rhetorical ploys). In all cases, our aim as translators is to make our texts read like originals—well-written English originals—that sound natural and are effective in conveying the author's meaning.

Readability can best be achieved through flexibility of approach, by testing out different English versions. This practice, which will eventually become automatic, should soon lead to greater freedom in the translation process.

These aims are interrelated, and so are the difficulties translators often encounter. That is why many of the examples that follow offer more than one solution, some better than others. There is seldom only one right translation (and usually a few wrong ones as well). A serious, attentive approach to the original text, supported by a developing sense of freedom, will eventually lead to self-confidence and pride in your work. This is quite different from a dangerously carefree attitude, when self-confidence becomes hubris. While a serious attitude does not exclude rapid intuitive translation, it does demand a thorough job of self-editing.

An important question for the translator is the intended readership. Is this author writing for professionals, for young people, for the general reading public? Professionals tend to communicate with one another in a kind of shorthand made up of special terms that, say, readers of popular science who are not physicists or biologists might find hard to decipher. If a text is written for professionals ("insiders"), terminology should not be tampered with, but syntax can definitely be changed to make the text more readable. For a popular text, the trick is to clearly and carefully convey any jargon in plain though not necessarily layman's English. In all cases the cultural factor must be taken into account, since a lack of sensitivity on the translator's part can lead to major misunderstanding and distortion of the author's intent.

Note: For the sake of simplicity, "the translator" here will be referred to as "he." So will "the author" and "the reader."

STARTING OUT – A FRAMEWORK FOR ANALYSIS

Hints on "how to" and "how not to" must start with pre-translation scanning. Your text is now in front of you. Instead of rushing to translate the first sentence, and on to the next and the next, trying to solve every problem on the spot, first pause and reflect:

1. What is this text about? To find out, you have to read a good chunk ahead, if not the whole thing.

2. For whom do you believe the text was originally intended? For readers in the U.S.? For a Russian audience?

3. Is the tone of the text straightforward, officialese, purple prose, journalistic, informal, conversational, familiar, tongue-in-cheek, or something else? Would this style correspond to, or be appropriate for, an original text in English?

4. Does it seem to have a particular agenda (is it favorable or unfavorable in tone)? How do you intend to put this across?

5. Does the author always mean what he seems to be saying?

CHAPTER 2

THE TRANSLATION PROCESS

Translation work is usually seen as consisting of three stages: 1) studying the original, 2) the translation work proper, and 3) self-editing. Yet so many students and professionals believe they can dispense with the first stage and the last one, leaving only the middle, the "interesting" one, to pursue. A sub-stage within all three might be labeled "collecting information." Practice in noticing and classifying difficulties should cut down on the time required for dealing with the Russian text at Stage 1. And Stage 3 sometimes proves to be the most enjoyable!

Naturally, to translate a Russian text into English, you must understand the original—in depth. This may seem like superfluous advice, but many of us, especially if we have formed a general impression of the meaning and are rushing to meet a deadline, tend to heedlessly proceed to the actual translation, ignoring cues in the Russian that might point the way to a real understanding of the text.

As you study sections of the original Russian, try to determine the overall sense, but remain alert to individual words and phrases that raise questions in your mind. This could be the time to consult available resources (print or online). Methods of using them may involve some trekking back and forth for hints as to meaning and usage in a particular context. A clue in a Russian-English dictionary, then on to a Webster's, an English-Russian dictionary, a dictionary of Russian synonyms, a Roget or another thesaurus might provide a lead in the direction you need. An unsuccessful search may propel you to one of the "tricks of the translator's trade," such as the antonymic translation, a conversive re-arrangement, or the tactic of generalization.

If after you have puzzled over the text and done some dictionary research, the Russian is still unclear, it is time to examine the grammar of the original more closely, to clarify relationships between sentence elements. Break down the particular sentence into its components, matching subject to verb, and locating and identifying secondary and auxiliary units. Watch out for prepositions, including those embedded in a verb, because the obvious or "natural" equivalent that springs to mind is not always the right one in English. Verb tenses and aspects can be treacherous, and so can case endings. All of these require constant attention.

If the meaning of a passage still eludes you, consider the possibility that this may in fact be a stereotyped expression conveying no substantially new information. Or it may be an idiom, a figure of speech, or a symbolic or hidden reference to some other text known to many Russians, or an event or television program that a Russian reader would easily recognize. Here the Internet or a colleague or expert on that subject may prove to be the best resource.

Finally, to grasp the meaning of the Russian original and make the translation conform to accepted standards for vocabulary and collocations ("what goes with what in English?"), outside information may be required. Unless the original Russian text is on a familiar subject, there may be a need to seek out original (not translated) English material in print or online. The background this provides may help you move closer to the meaning of the problematic Russian words and supply the needed vocabulary items.

Since the literal meaning of some very high-frequency Russian words and stereotyped phrases has been gradually eroded through overuse, the translator's first task is always to truly understand what the intent was in the original Russian. The idea is not just to find a particular word; that is only the first step. You will have to differentiate between variations in the meaning of lexical units that constantly pop up in Russian so that you can zero in on the English that goes best with the rest of the sentence, perhaps opting for an entire makeover of the sentence structure.

Grasping the Russian thought, especially one expressed clumsily, with heavy, convoluted syntax and stereotyped expressions, presents a challenge for the thoughtful translator. Among the most difficult texts are those containing approximate formulations, mostly noun-based, with vague "all-purpose" verbs and passive or impersonal constructions, with clause leading into clause and phrase interrupting phrase.

As you begin reading the Russian text, not yet translating, you will be taking in the information each sentence contains. This provides an initial impression of what the author has to say. Even at this early stage though, think about how to convey the thought behind the author's words. Since the original Russian is likely to call to mind at least the dictionary equivalents, try to assess the potential effect of this "draft translation" on the reader, and mentally begin making the necessary adjustments. Later, there will be time to decide whether to stop at every doubtful spot or forge ahead—that is a personal choice. In either case, there are bound to be places that prove genuinely baffling, and not only to a beginner. Some translators want to start troubleshooting then and there; others prefer to read ahead so as to tackle these difficulties later on. The main thing at this stage is not to rush too quickly into "translation mode," and never to forget the crucial importance of context, both when looking over the original Russian (individual words and larger units) and when translating into English. Context can help you decide on *form*, on what words to choose and how to arrange them to best convey the sense. Judging when and how you can change *content* is a different, but equally important matter. The context, your background knowledge, and possible information on the intended readership, will contribute to that judgment.

FORM AND FUNCTION

In analyzing the Russian original, start with the form that you see in the text and look for the function that shaped it. For a viable alternative to merely translating words, take the function you have discovered in the original and give it a new form in English.

One way to recognize function in the Russian is to break up the sentence into sense units. Don't automatically reach for the dictionary equivalent of each word, using the same part of speech as the Russian original.

Another way is to treat the entire sentence as a single unified whole, so that you can restate the author's thought yourself. This method obviates the need to consider each word separately. And though the form in the translation may look very different from the form in the original, see that the author's message remains intact.

When a Russian sentence seems somehow to read backwards or inside out, first try to rearrange the components in a more familiar order, e.g., as "subject-verb-object."

Победой бастующих завершилась 4-недельная забастовка. Рабочие добились повышения заработной платы, лучших условий труда.
or
В результате 4-недельной забастовки рабочие добились повышения заработной платы, лучших условий труда.

A four-week long strike has ended in victory for the workers, who got pay increases and better working conditions as a result.

While that should make it simpler to identify key and secondary units, it definitely does not mean you must stick to this interim order when translating, e.g.:

Strikers can now celebrate the end of a four-week-long walkout, after winning concessions on most of their demands.

Strikers can now celebrate the end of a four-week-long walkout, as their demands for higher pay and better conditions were finally met.

If there is a prepositional phrase at the start of the Russian sentence, or its equivalent expressed as a noun in an oblique case, give it a temporary place in the simplified "generic" sentence structure or look for a key word to re-site the same way. This technique is meant to help you focus on the thought in the sentence and encourage further experimentation.

By now you can begin to translate. Never, however, try to tackle words individually without due regard for the context. Better a rendering of the idea as a whole than a faithful "dictionary" reproduction of each of the words, strung together as on a clothesline. No reader will thank you for such fidelity—and neither would the author.

Some translators believe that the process of translation is simpler than what we have outlined here, that theory and procedures for translation are not really necessary, or can more profitably be studied in a classroom. Naturally, when you are already working on a translation, that is no time to start theorizing, and many translators virtually unacquainted with theory still manage to produce adequate translations by simply following their noses. With or without a theoretical background, however, it is important to 1) study lists of signals to watch out for in the source language, 2) "hear" (and heed) the alarm bells when you edit your translation, and 3) make consideration of potential variants so automatic that this becomes an integral part of your translation work.

Every piece of writing, both in the original Russian and in translation, has its distinctive form, designed to express the author's ideas. How well they come across to the non-Russian reader depends on how closely the translation is linked to the thoughts in the original. The translator who is not tied to a word-for-word rendering instinctively looks for the gist of a sentence to clarify for himself the function of each component (in the Russian) before deciding on the form (in English). Though he may have to dig through a lot of verbiage to come up with the function, once he has found it and deciphered the text accordingly, he has also found freedom— the translator's freedom to recreate the author's thought in English.

It is the translator's job to understand not only the author's individual words, but his intention as well, then express the whole in the clearest and most attractive way possible. For each component, or all of them taken together, three aspects can normally be identified:

1. Its role in the sentence/paragraph ("what structural category does it belong to, and how does it contribute to expressing the thought?")

2. The raison d'être of the component/sentence ("what is the thought anyway?")

3. Its underlying "agenda," or attitude, whether clearly articulated or implied ("how does the author feel about it?")

Many problems connected with these aspects are themselves connected and can therefore be tackled together. For each component, as for the sentence as a whole, there may be more than one way to communicate a thought. The translator should seek out the relevant semantic field, or menu of related words, and sift through the available options for putting together the words he chooses, trying one version after another until the most effective one has emerged, continuing this way all through the portion being translated. After that, ideally, he should put the translation aside and look at it the next day with a fresh eye (and a fresh ear if read aloud) to catch such flaws as unintentional repetition of words or sounds, and a crowded, unbalanced or excessively long sentence. He can then edit, hone, and polish the draft text while consulting the resources at his command until he is satisfied with the result.

What then stands behind the sentences on the page before us? What role do the different components play, structurally and semantically? If we are to translate the author's ideas rather than merely producing an equivalent for every Russian word he wrote, we must give thought to the specific function of these words.

HINTS ON PROCEDURE

Read all or a good way ahead in the Russian original for background, to get an idea of the import and general tone (straightforward, emotional, ironical, playful) and possible help from the context (the use of a word again in a different case, a different collocation, or even an actual explanation).

Lexical aspect. Be wary of what are sometimes called "false friends of the translator," including cognates (words with a common or related root) and calques (loan translations), and also the first entry in the Russian-English dictionary (though occasionally this may turn out to be the only possible option or even an effective solution). And remember that in different contexts high-frequency Russian words may have a wide variety of meanings.

Syntactic aspect. At first, treat Russian syntax as an aid to comprehension, then disregard it while seeking the most effective English version. Unless you are going to be a slave to the Russian form, changes in the syntax of the translation will be inevitable. Be aware of the grammar of the original Russian sentence, but translate according to the rules of English. In the target language, "usage is king." As an English speaker, you can let a sensitive ear be your guide. Read the text aloud, for listening to your own translation can help catch many an awkward word choice or sequence.

CHANGING CONTENT

Make changes when you have the right or duty to do so (and don't when you do not):

1. To provide an unobtrusive explanation
2. To leave out a non-essential item, including unnecessary repetition
3. To properly handle perceived hyperbole/exaggeration
4. To bring loaded words in line with the author's intention
5. To give more credibility to titles, headlines, and leads, or make them more eye-catching
6. To deal with residual sovietisms, leftovers of the Marxist-Leninist era that crop up not solely in political texts, words and collocations that have imperceptibly become part of the Russian language.

If a Russian title, heading, or headline does not convey the author's intent, or is so flat and uninspiring as to discourage a potential reader from venturing into the text, it is better to change it, borrowing words from the body of the text or even completely transforming it.

When words have become desemanticized (meaning eroded) from overuse in Russian, any alteration in the translation needs to be approached gingerly, allowing the author's bias to come through.

CHAPTER 3

Accuracy – The Essence of Translation

This book attempts to point out ways in which the translator can convey the intention of the author of an original Russian text so that an American reader might react to the translation in the same way as the Russian reader would react to the original, i.e., understand it the same way.

Clearly, such criteria go far beyond the usual demand that the translation be "true and correct" or "absolutely accurate." (Some clients are even naïve enough to compare the number of words in the Russian and English versions, and to insist that these match up!)

Yet accuracy is not merely an important consideration—it is key. The challenge lies in how to achieve true accuracy without sacrificing readability or good English usage.

What Makes a Translation Accurate?

The first thing to do is identify what is important in the original sentence or paragraph—important to the author, that is. Once you find those key words, the translation will begin to take shape on its own. Without this first step, it will be just a collection of signs with no map and no driving directions. But a good translator can steer his readers through a text smoothly and reliably.

Key words vs. props

In order to determine how (or if) a word should be translated, prime consideration should be given to whether that word in a particular Russian sentence is a key word or an auxiliary (prop). This, rather than a "faithful" rendition of each word on an equal basis, would go a long way to making the translation accurate. (Note that prepositions, as organizers, are important auxiliaries.) To put it another way, would the sentence still mean essentially the same thing without the word in question, or is it truly indispensable?

Take the word явление. If the sentence speaks of негативные явления в экономике, then "trial by deletion" will demonstrate that явления here is only a prop word for негативные, which should be playing the leading role. Possible options, besides "*on the negative side, the economy (is) …*" might include "*adverse features of the economy.*" Aside from grammatical considerations, therefore, негативное in this case could stand alone as far as the sense is concerned.

But in the case that follows, the word целое cannot stand by itself. It means nothing without явление, though явление alone would be understandable. Thus, in Шаляпин—это целое явление в искусстве, it is явление that bears the main thrust of the meaning. The translation of явление should therefore correspond to its status in the sentence: "*Chaliapin was a phenomenon in the world of art.*" If testing this by deletion proves inconclusive, you could experiment with paraphrasing and/or compression. As in: "*The phenomenal Russian bass Chaliapin was a master of expressive vocal color.*" This combines the original sentence with the one that follows.

Take another case using явление. Is it key (essential) here, or prop (supporting)?

> Заявлять о том, что ядерный удар—это возможное, допустимое явление указывает не просто на безответственность, а прямо на безумие.
> To declare that a nuclear strike is possible, something that can, or should, be allowed to happen, is not just irresponsible—it is madness.

Here, the noun явление is a prop for the two adjectives, возможное and допустимое, that only appear to modify it. Our trial by deletion (or substitution of a generalized term, here the word "something") once again demonstrates this.

Let's try a different prop. Is it really a prop, though? Perhaps it needs only to be tweaked to become meaningful.

> В историческом плане проблемы, которые мы сегодня относим к числу глобальных возникли и получили развитие на почве эксплуататорского строя.
> Historically, problems we now see as global got their start and developed in exploitative societies.

The initial adverbial phrase with the prop word плане can conveniently be replaced by a one-word adverb, which will achieve a shorter, punchier delivery, particularly when на почве—a true prop here—is also deleted. The same holds true for к числу, which was necessary only as a grammatical adjunct to относим.

> Автор останавливается на узловых (вопросах) (характеристики) шаманизма.
> (Author) Vitebsky examines some of the essential features of shamanism.

As the words underlined above show, the frequency with which certain words are used in Russian and in English differs greatly. Автор here could also be replaced by the writer's name. Останавливается, instead of the dated and overused *"dwells on,"* can be rendered by a more specific verb, here *"examines."* Вопросах supplies no essential information in either the English or the Russian, so is best omitted. In Russian it is sometimes used as a prop word for grammatical reasons, for balance, or simply by inertia. Finally, характеристика really means характер, but again, it turns out to be redundant.

> В справочнике <u>на</u> большом фактическом <u>материале</u> раскрывается
> сущность современной внешней политики.
> An abundance of facts exposes the *essence / very core* of *our / their / (a
> country's)* foreign policy today.

A problem preposition, на, need not be translated if the sentence is recast. And when материал is recognized as pseudo-significant and not a key word, it can also be omitted in English. *"Reference book"* may be dropped if mentioned in preceding sentences. Note the change from the reflexive раскрывается to the active *"exposes"* as more direct.

"Process nouns" as props
Watch out for the pesky process nouns derived from verbs, especially the seemingly ever-present ones ending in -ание / -ение. Though similar to English verbal nouns, process nouns are often not needed in the translation.

   To ensure accuracy as well as ease in reading, one possibility is to take a more direct approach, turning a combination such as "prop verb + process noun" into a finite verb or another part of speech. The prop verb is often a multi-purpose verb functioning solely as a necessary grammatical adjunct with the process noun, e.g., осуществлять управление. But instead of the translation *"implement (the) management of"* (not quite English), a better choice would be *"provide managerial services,"* or even just *"manage."*

> Была отмечена совместная озабоченность <u>торможением</u> (прогресса)
> переговоров по <u>улаживанию</u> конфликта, что вызвало растущую угрозу
> нового всплеска насилия.
> Both sides noted with anxiety the hold-up in the talks aimed at settling the
> conflict, (which was) increasing the threat of another outbreak of violence.
> *or*
> Concern was voiced by both parties over the slow-down of/in the
> reconciliation talks that could lead to further violence.

> <u>углубление</u> педагогической подготовки
> <u>providing better</u> professional grounding
> a <u>sound</u> professional basis for the would-be teacher

Take one example without an –ание suffix, сушка, as in: сушку производить в специальной камере. Instead of translating as *"do/perform/carry out the drying ...,"* (unidiomatic), one could simply use the imperative, *"dry the material."* Variants might be: *"Drying takes place in a separate chamber"*; or with a passive construction: *"The (material) is dried in a separate chamber."*

Identify a process noun in the original Russian, change the part of speech if necessary, and move words around as needed to find the best position for this word in the English sentence. Don't be thrown off if a prop momentarily obscures the key word. Look for that key word and go on from there.

проблема (обеспечения) безопасности
the security problem; how to guarantee security

Это снижает вероятность (возникновения) трудовых конфликтов.
This reduces / This cuts down (on) the possibility of conflicts (arising) between labor and management.
or
This makes disputes (erupting) between labor and management less likely.

Use your judgment on whether or not to translate the -ения process noun itself or one with a different form:

(Реализация) системы мер, (направленных) на (предоставление) помощи гражданам с малым доходом призвана снизить рост преступности в городе.
(A system of) measures *(aimed at) aiding / to aid* low-income families/citizens is/are meant/expected to bring down (the) crime (rate) in the city.

(Приведение) в силу программы будет способствовать снижению преступности в городе.
When the program becomes operational there will/should be a <u>drop</u> in the crime rate.
When the program goes into force we will see a <u>drop</u> in the crime rate.
With the program in force, there will/should be a <u>drop</u> in the crime rate.

(Сосредоточить/внимание) преподавателей на (повышение) успеваемости.
Teachers <u>must focus</u> on (improving) student performance.

All -ание's, of course, are not created equal. Внимание, for example, is a noun, pure and simple. True, it was originally derived from the verb внимать/внять (*to hark/listen/heed*), but has since lost its "process" function, while the verb itself survives in only a few collocations. The word повышение in the illustration above is still able to "process," but the translation need not necessarily reflect that, because with or without the word *"improving,"* the sentence still means the same.

Необходим научно <u>обоснованный</u> подход / Необходимо выработать научно <u>обоснованный</u> подход / к нормиров<u>анию</u> выбросов загрязняющих веществ с <u>учетом</u> приоритет<u>ности</u> и / а также к нормиров<u>анию</u> использов<u>ания</u> природных ресурсов.

Worse: A scientifically substantiated approach to the regulation of the dis charge of pollutants based on a system of priorities and to control over the exploitation of natural resources is necessary.

Better: A system of priorities *must be (scientifically) worked out / is needed* to regulate the discharge of pollutants and set standards to regulate/control/manage the use of natural resources.

A Russian sentence beginning with a "process noun," if the word order is carried over into the translation, makes a poor showing in English. And by interfering with the way the reader in a hurry perceives the author's idea—drawing his attention away from the words with the main message (the "raison d'être")—the overused process nouns detract from the accuracy of the translation. Even if not in the -ание form, such a noun in an oblique case can make life harder for the translator, but not if he remembers to change that noun to the subject (in the nominative case), or to convert it to another part of speech (re-verbalize, perhaps), and then give it the spot it deserves in the translation.

<u>Анализу</u> современного состояния основных направлений и тенденций развития <u>экономических</u> <u>отношений</u> между социалистическими и капиталистическими странами посвящено недавно вышедшее <u>исследование</u>.

Here it is not only the initial process noun that makes this sentence so difficult. The key words are separated by a mass of verbiage, and yet the key to the translation lies precisely in that "verbiage." The key words can come first:

A <u>study</u> just out *analyses / looks at* <u>economic relations</u> between socialist and capitalist countries today and examines trends of development.
or
<u>Economic relations</u> between socialist and capitalist states today ... are the subject of a <u>study</u> just released.

Some props are nouns that do not require translation:

(<u>интересы</u>) мира требуют ...
peace requires/demands ...

они борются за (<u>дело</u>) мира
they are (constantly) campaigning for peace; (make a) stand (up) for peace;
  do everything they can for peace

Some props are verbs that can also be dropped:

<u>наносить</u> вред/ удар
to hurt/harm/damage/hit (a reputation, an organization, etc.)

Although "*to inflict* + *harm/damage*" is also acceptable, do not use props automatically.

<u>терпеть</u> аварию	to be in an accident; to have an accident
<u>терпеть</u> провал	to fail; to lose (out); to bomb (*where slang is not inappropriate*)
<u>терпеть</u> унижение	to be humiliated

Предложение будет встречено с интересом, получит <u>широкую</u>
  поддержку …
or
… <u>обязательно</u> вызовет интерес, как у большого бизнеса, так и у
  широкой общественности.
The proposal is <u>sure</u> to win broad support, and will be of interest to big
  business and the <u>public</u> at large.
or
Big business will be interested and so will the consumers/investors/public
  (<u>as a whole</u>).

Context dictates how specific the translation should be. Extra words in English (*sure, great, at large*) compensate here for the loss of the dictionary equivalents of широкую and обязательно and facilitate the rhythmic flow of the thought, providing end weight for balance. These are all ways to help our "customer," the reader, get through our translation. The second version can omit "*proposal*" because it is clear from the context.

Props partnering key words
When a vague and weak Russian "all-purpose" verb, noun, or other part of speech taken by itself would send only an insignificant message, look for a nearby key word that carries the principal semantic load. Then consider it in context. Immediately recognizing such a verb as a prop makes it easy to spot its partner, the key word that so often follows it. Such desemanticized words or phrases have lost much of their meaning through overuse and tend to be ignored by the Russian

reader, but sound unacceptably obtrusive in English translation. Take (or rather, get rid of) вызывать, as in вызывать возмущение/недовольство. Instead of the tired old standby, *"evoke indignation"* (and most contexts would call for a stronger English noun anyway), highlight the underlying category of *"cause."* Possible solutions include:

- substituting the key word for the original collocation, but as a verb: *to anger, to infuriate, to enrage, etc.*

- combining the key word with another, more semantically specific verbal partner: *to arouse anger/indignation*, or even *to kindle it, set it off, provoke it*, or *touch it off*

- coupling the key word or a derivative with a common English verb: *make somebody angry*; *move somebody to anger*

- employing the translator's tactic of conversion by shifting the "actors" around, while adjusting the rest of the sentence: *They responded with anger*; *Their reaction was (one of) anger*; *An angry response greeted this proposal*

Or take an example where the solution depends on whether the key noun has a modifier that is also key:

проводить (предвыборную) кампанию

If the noun кампанию is the key word, проводить is only a prop, better converted to a verb that can stand alone: *"to campaign."* But when it is the organizational part of the campaign that is being highlighted, then it is better to spell it all out: *"organize/put together/think out a campaign."*

проводить опрос общественного мнения в Нью-Йорке
instead of: conduct a public opinion poll in New York
try: to poll New Yorkers

проводить перекрестный допрос свидетеля
to cross-examine a witness

заниматься вымогательством
instead of: engage in blackmail
try: to blackmail somebody; extort something/money; to be a blackmailer/ extortionist

For other Russian "auxiliary" ("prop") verbs, e.g., совершать, допускать, осуществлять, use an English verb commonly paired with the specific noun in English:

совершить преступление   commit a crime

допустить ошибку   make a mistake
(*also*: ошибиться)

Or once again, as before, combine into just the one verb:

осуществлять контроль (*also*: контролировать)
monitor; supervise; (*rarely*) control

осуществлять руководство (проекта) (*also*: руководить)
manage; head (a project, etc.)

осуществлять руководство (агентства / ведомства / фирмы)
  (*also*: руководить)
lead; guide; head; run an agency/company

проводить/ставить опыты/эксперименты
to experiment (*reserving*: perform/conduct/engage in experimentation)

In texts where a key noun used with the prop verb проводить is modified, as in:

провел множество опытов
performed numerous experiments; ran a whole series of tests

translate the combination as is, prop verb and all.

проводить урок also: преподавать (*intransitive*)
teach a class/lesson (during a class period); teach (be a teacher/professor)

производить подсчет (*also*: подсчитывать)
count; calculate; estimate; total

производить ремонт (квартиры) (*also*: ремонтировать)
renovate; repair
but:
производить (капитальный) ремонт жилого дома (автомобиля)
remodel; do major repairs; overhaul; recondition (a house/apartment/car)

обращаться с призывом
appeal to/for; call for/on someone (to do something)

обращаться к словарю
look it up

обращаться за помощью
ask/appeal for help

Certain stereotyped expressions, including prepositional phrases (semi-operators) and expressions of time, are closely related to props. In a sentence containing: <u>в условиях</u> резкого / <u>нарастающего</u> обострения международной обстановки, since the tone is far from neutral, instead of *"in conditions of,"* weigh the possibility of using: *"in the face of ..."* Another option is to simply use *"with ... +* a participle,"* as in: *"with relations rapidly worsening."* The following versions would also work:

... <u>at a time</u> when international relations are rapidly deteriorating
or
... <u>as</u> (relations) grow sharply worse
or even
... are obviously going downhill ...

Here the participial phrase is tacked on to the principal clause. Naturally, a colloquial expression will do only if it is compatible with the tone of the original text.

Усиливается негативное <u>отношение</u> к данной политике.
or
Растет недовольство по отношению к такой политике.
or
Растет недовольство по отношению к этой политике / в связи с этой
   политикой.
Opposition to these policies is growing.

Ему тесно <u>в рамках</u> наших устоявшихся традиций.
He feels hemmed in by our long-established traditions.
To him our traditions seem stifling.

In addition to their basic meaning, words such as дело or вопрос have in many contexts become mere props, devoid of nearly any meaning and requiring a key word as a "partner" to make sense. When used together with such a key word, e.g., "Всегда будем бороться за (<u>дело</u>) мира" *"We shall fight for peace, no matter what,"* дело is redundant. Or take:

Мы здесь сегодня собрались, чтобы обсудить <u>вопрос</u> о незаконных
   увольнениях.
We are here today to discuss the illegal firings.

К <u>вопросу</u> о кредите/(<u>предоставлении</u>) кредита ...
About (extending) credit ...

Should a "prop-plus-key-word" combination always be condensed, or always translated as is? Actually, there is no cut-and-dried solution—everything depends on context.

If выдвинуть is read as a unit, "*propose*" alone will do, but if the phrase reads выдвинуть интересное предложение, it would make sense to retain the entire combination, perhaps as: "*bring an interesting proposal to the table*" or "*submit an exciting proposal.*"

Прилагать усилия	to try
but with:	
Прилагать огромные усилия	to make *a great / an enormous* effort
Выразить надежду	to hope

Even with ... искреннюю надежду, it could still translate as "*sincerely hope*"; otherwise: "*express (our) sincere hope,*" with the syntax adjusted to properly render the sentence.

In cases where дело, вопрос, or other high-frequency items act as key words rather than prop words, they cannot be omitted in translation. For example:

В прошлом году он открыл собственное дело.
Last year he started his own business.

"Ну, а это уж мое дело!" (*indicating an indignant reaction*)
"(*Well / You know,*) that (just) happens to be <u>my</u> business!"
"(Look,) Mind your own business!"

Some competent Russian editors eliminate these superfluous words in the original texts, and tone down the bombast, because many Russian readers are exasperated by pompous, stereotyped, pseudo-scientific, or simply careless writing. Today the situation has improved somewhat; the lofty rhetoric has receded, giving way to a deliberately matter-of-fact, and even colloquial style frequently found in the press. Occasionally, conversational "asides" appear in what used to be consistently formal texts, such as political speeches.

Identifiers – when do we need them?

Do we translate identifiers? The answer is not always. An identifier, "label," or "tag," with a function halfway between a prop and a modifier, may help the reader understand an unfamiliar term or name. Other times, it is needed only in the Russian.

У дверей стоял новенький (<u>автомобиль</u>) (<u>марки</u>) "Сатурн".
Outside stood a neat little Saturn.

As a matter of fact, a Мерседес or a БМВ (*BMW*) could easily stand alone in Russian, without the identifier марки, as imports like these are easily recognized. Such cultural details also factor into the translator's job.

Consider leaving out other identifiers where they serve little purpose in English:

Во время службы, (слово) "аминь" повторяется множество раз, как подтверждение сказанного.
And "amen," signifying agreement with the words that precede it, is heard numerous times during the service.

... переводя рабочую силу из сельского хозяйства в <u>сферу</u> промышленности и услуг
… transferring workforce from agriculture to manufacturing and services

When we see специалист в области (чего-то), or работает в (какой-то) области, we recognize that the word for "*area*" or "*field*" is an identifier and should probably be dispensed with:

специалист <u>в области</u> ракетно-космической техники
a rocket scientist; a space engineer

… в (<u>области</u>) математики
… in mathematics

The word for "*field*" is easily omitted above, but in в этой области (*in this field/area*) the word is key and must not be omitted. In the next example, области is also needed for the sense:

В какой <u>области</u> его вклад наиболее значителен?
In what <u>field</u> was his contribution the greatest?
<u>Where</u> did he do his most significant work?

The need for an identifier depends on the context and who the text is meant for:

То, что требуется, это экономичные двигатели, у которых <u>одновременно</u> резко снижен <u>объем</u> токсичных выбросов <u>в атмосферу</u>.
What is needed is an engine that <u>combines</u> economy with a sharp reduction in toxic exhaust.

On the other hand, many Russian words, names, and concepts do need identifiers in a translation, or even full-fledged explanations. This occurs when a word, phrase, or concept is so unfamiliar to the American reader that it requires addi tional words to clarify the author's thought. In this example, the Russian word i transliterated, then explained as well: гласность would be "*glasnost, the new openness/transparency.*" This term gained currency in the Gorbachev era, though предавать гласности (*make public*) existed in various contexts before that and is very popular today.

Эти строки посвящены Жуковскому.
These verses were <u>dedicated</u> to the <u>Russian poet</u> Zhukovsky.

For another meaning of посвящены, one would be guided by the context, a below:

These lines are / This part is <u>about</u> Vassily Zhukovsky, the <u>19th-century Romantic poet</u>.

На Чукотском полуострове издавна живут эскимосы и чукчи.
The Chukchi and the Eskimo have lived <u>for thousands of years</u> on the Chukotka Peninsula <u>in the Russian Far East</u>. (*unobtrusive explanation*)

Название «кремль» <u>появилось</u> в XIV веке, хотя сама крепость <u>появилась</u> раньше.
The word кремль "*kremlin*" (Russian for citadel or fortress) first appeared ir the fourteenth century, but by that time, the fortress itself was already there.

Where repetition (появилось … появилась) would serve no useful purpose ir English, look for a substitute.

Сайгаков в настоящее время насчитывается не менее 20.000 особей.
Популяция их восстановилась к середине 20-го века.
The saigaks in Russia now number at least 20,000. Populations of <u>this migrating sheep-like antelope</u> recovered by the mid-twentieth century.

The phrase (известный) композитор Арам Хачатурян should be translated as "*the composer Khachaturian,*" or "*Khachaturian, the composer,*" or with no identifier at all if the context is about classical composers anyway, or say, com posers in the Soviet Union. Compare this with "*a well-known composer,*" which would signal that if he must be introduced thus, you probably never heard of him so he couldn't be very important. Both the indefinite article, as used in the variant, and the literal translation of известный would conspire to make that clear. Moral: to avoid giving the wrong impression, don't do word-for-word.

Going back to the opposite case, when the Russian author is identifying a name or concept already known to readers in the U.S., e.g., известный американский композитор К. Портер, this should be just *"Cole Porter,"* without *"the well-known American composer."* Sadly, in our day, with some of the most memorable artists all but forgotten, знаменитый итальянский тенор Карузо would probably have to remain as *"the great Italian tenor Enrico Caruso."* And no initials please: we don't say *"R. Reagan"* or *"G. Bush"* as a Russian writer might, though Russians do tend to use an initial or initials (for name and patronymic) with a Russian name. The exception for an English name would be if the form of that name, as in E.M. Forster, is the accepted one, because *"Edward Morgan Forster"* would simply not be recognized. The same with Gerbert Dzhordzh Uells—people would just have to guess at who that might be.

Organizers to orient the reader

Whether as operators, semi-operators, or transitions, organizers help arrange the sentence and paragraph so that readers may more easily find their way around a translated text. This category includes prepositions, phrases that function as prepositions (semi-operators), and certain conjunctions. But to utilize the English equivalents of the Russian organizer most efficiently, the translator needs to be prepared to paraphrase.

Это удастся сделать только с помощью нового устройства.

The translation need not always be *"with the help of"*—there are other options:

This can be done only *with* / *by using* the new device.
Without it, the process will not work.
It will take that new contraption to do the trick.

Or take a sentence that seems to require *"in the course of"* but other solutions also beg to be considered, say:

В ходе разбирательства выяснилось, что ...
During the investigation, it was found that ...

Or even a sentence totally recast, with the Russian reflexive transformed into an English active:

The investigation revealed that ...

Now take the following:

(В условиях) такой системы возникает ...
Under such a system ...

Or perhaps even omit, as in:
Such a system gives rise to ...

(В условиях) кризиса / В кризисных условиях необходимо ...
During this crisis; In a crisis (situation)
Or omit, as in:
The crisis (itself) makes it necessary to ...

SENSE CATEGORIES: THE MAIN THRUST

The challenge for the translator is to ferret out the logic of the Russian sentence, which would make it possible to see the relationship of the individual words to the overall reasoning behind those words, taken as a whole.

Cause – "how come ...?"

For this category, the words in the original express action that results in, or leads to, some effect.

В результате нападения погибли сотни мирных жителей ...
or
Нападение привело к гибели ...
The raid *killed* hundreds of civilians / *left* hundreds of civilians *dead* /
  claimed hundreds of *lives*.

В числе прочих факторов, безрассудная спекуляция на бирже привела к
  кризису / спровоцировала кризис тридцатых годов ...
Reckless stock market speculation was *among* the factors that *led to* /
  contributed to / *resulted in* the Great Depression of the 1930s ...

... и вплоть до начала Второй мировой войны царила невиданная ранее
  безработица.
... which gave rise to an unprecedented level of unemployment that lasted
  until the start of World War II.
or
... which took the country to a level of unemployment never before seen.
or
... and the country *was in the grip of* ... / *had to endure* ...

обусловлено/порождено/вызвано (чем-то) ...
brought on / about by ...; is responsible for ...

(что-то) обуславливает
gives rise to; breeds; leads to; engenders; ... springing (as it does) from ...

... положившего начало перестройке.
... which gave perestroika its start.

<u>Почему</u> вы так думаете?
What <u>makes</u> you think so?

<u>Безудержная</u> погоня за прибылью <u>обуславливает</u> <u>буквально</u>
<u>лавинообразное</u> нарастание противоречий.
The unrestrained/feverish/furious/frenzied pursuit of profit soon led to ...
Worse: snowballing tensions
Better: irreconcilable differences; discord

The unconvincing attempt to use a calque, or loan translation (though one not as strong as "*avalanche*"), i.e., "*snowballing tensions*" for буквально лавинооб-разное нарастание противоречий dooms the entire sentence. In the second example above, we have a more successful reflection of the expressive words in the original and the present tense in обуславливает, a tense jump that makes for even more emphasis in the Russian.

Purpose – "what for ...?"

Another test the translator can use in accessing the meaning behind the words of the original sentence, once again taken as a whole, involves looking for the reason behind the words chosen by the author: is there an expression of an aim/intention/motive?

Он вышел <u>погулять/покурить.</u>
He went out <u>for</u> a walk/smoke.

<u>Чтобы это достичь,</u> придется вложить большие капиталы и много лет
тяжелого труда.
For this / *To achieve* this you will need to invest a lot of money and years of
very hard work.
<u>To get this done</u> will take a lot of money and steady slogging over the years.

В целях упорядочения передвижения персонала ...
To / *In order to* / *So as to* facilitate employee traffic ...
To / *In order to* / *So as to* better organize the transport of employees ...

Сделай это <u>для</u> меня!
Do it (just) for me!

Приду. Хотя бы для того, <u>чтобы</u> лишний раз взглянуть на него.
I'll be there, if only to get another look at him.

Он это сделал (для того), чтобы ей было приятно.
He did it <u>to</u> *please her / make her happy.*

Приходи <u>на</u> обед, с нами покушаешь. (*Note: watch for run-on sentences.*)
Come for dinner. / Have dinner with us.

Задание на завтра …
The homework (for tomorrow) …

… <u>ради</u> продолжения рода
… not to allow the species to die out

<u>Ради чего</u> / <u>С какой целью</u> / <u>Зачем</u> вы все это затеяли?
What did you <u>want</u> to achieve?
<u>Why</u> did you start all this?
<u>What</u> did you do it <u>for</u>?

(*Note the excited, even aggravated tone of the questions both above and below.*)

И <u>к чему</u> все эти хлопоты?
<u>What's</u> all this (feverish activity) for?

Here, the hint of displeasure and even sarcasm in the Russian question should definitely be conveyed in the translation. The answer (which follows) is all innocence. The entire exchange in Russian calls for the same informal approach in English.

Мы <u>готовились</u> к празднику.
We were (just) <u>getting ready</u> for the holiday.

Contrast – "yes, but …"

Does the thought in the sentence indicate some type of opposition? Once the underlying idea is recognized, it is not difficult to find an appropriate English equivalent—without worrying about each individual word.

вместе с тем … / в то же время …
yet …; in spite of all that …; that said, …

The next example, в то же время, illustrates an exception because it is used in its basic meaning, connected with time and concurrent action.

А мы-то <u>в то время</u> были (уже) далеко.
or
А мы же к тому времени / <u>в то время</u> были (уже) далеко.

By that time, we were far away. (*concurrent action*)
But we were already <u>miles</u> away. (*depending on context*)

Contrast may be achieved by using various forms of emphasis.

(<u>Но</u>) вы <u>же</u> сами были <u>за</u>!
You were <u>all</u> for it at the time, <u>weren't you</u>?

Both the question form and the intensifier, "*all*," help put across the **Но**, the **же**, and the abruptly ending sentence structure of the Russian, sharpening the emphasis.

(<u>Так</u>) вам (<u>все таки</u>) надо было признать, что вы сами голосовали за это.
Then you should have admitted that you yourself voted for it.

<u>А вот теперь</u> вы говорите, что идея не годится.
<u>Now</u> you <u>claim</u> the idea won't work.

<u>Хоть</u> он и новичок в этом деле, сразу видно, на что он горазд/способен.
He <u>may</u> be new at *this job* / *this kind of thing*, but you can see right away
  what he *can do* / *is capable of*.

<u>А</u> она-<u>то</u> о чем тогда думала?
And what was <u>she</u> thinking at the time, <u>may I ask</u>?

Such a caustic comment could be added if justified by the context:

<u>С другой стороны</u>, вам не кажется, что он просто искусно врет?
Wouldn't you say he's just an accomplished liar?
He sure knows how to twist the truth, doesn't he?
What a prevaricator!

<u>Однако</u>, я тоже чувствую, (что) тут что-то не то.
I <u>myself</u> feel that something *is not what it seems* / *is not right* / *is fishy*.

(<u>И все же</u>) я лично считаю, (что) здесь нечего бояться.
(I don't know, but) I <u>personally</u> believe there is nothing to be afraid of.

<u>Несмотря</u> на то, что вы опоздали, идемте, я вас посажу.
You are late all right; come on, <u>though</u>, I'll find you a seat.

В глазах <u>иных</u> наблюдателей это похоже на прогресс.
В глазах <u>иных</u> наблюдателей это выглядит так, <u>как будто</u> дела идут на
  поправку.
Certain observers (however) see this as progress.
Certain observers (however) say it looks as if things are getting better.

The use of иных in this context lends an unfavorable tinge because it appears in so many articles with a negative outlook. Although in "Есть и иное / другое мнение," the word used as an adjective is neutral in tone.

Sometimes the English has no introduction at all, using only a simple negation, as in:

> Мы искали любые признаки раскаяния, <u>но</u> не нашли.
> We looked for any sign of remorse. There was none.

> Правда, было <u>не совсем так</u>, и даже <u>совсем не так</u>.
> <u>Actually</u>, it wasn't quite like that. In fact, not (at all) like that (at all).

Note the ironical twist occasioned by the play on words in the Russian, when the exact same words are turned the other way around. The translation can tackle the emphatic denial, but the irony is only implied, with compensation needed further along in the text.

Another version of the same idea in Russian would be:

> <u>В действительности</u>, дело обстояло как раз наоборот
> *or*
> <u>На деле (же)</u>, положение совсем иное

В действительности should not to be confused with действительно, which would signal agreement, not contrast. Any of the following versions would fit either of the Russian sentences above:

> *In actual fact* / *However* / *But* the situation was not like that (at all).
> <u>Actually</u>, it wasn't like that at all.
> Things were completely different.
> What happened was the exact opposite (of what he says).
> Facts (however) speak to the contrary.
> Well, he was wrong.

The first version does contain words indicating contrast, while in the second there is a choice as to whether or not to use any introduction, the stark option perhaps being the more effective. The fourth version is a total makeover (the "*he*" refers to a previous sentence in the context).

Negation – "just say no?"

The original may contain an instance of denial, stated or implied, with either more or less emphasis. A total makeover can be applied to any of these original examples. The main thing is to identify the negative content. From then on, it should be smooth sailing.

<u>Ни в коем случае</u> туда не ходи.
<u>Whatever you do</u>, don't go there.

<u>Ни за что</u> не пойду!
I wouldn't think of it!

А что будет если (все таки) пойду?
(But) what would happen if I did go?

Да ничего, только тебя поймает злой дядька, посадит в мешок и унесет.
  А потом еще съест.
Nothing, really. Only the bogey man will catch you, put you in his bag, take
  you away and eat you for supper.

Не любитель я такого рода веселья.
That doesn't sound like fun.

The fanciful examples above illustrate various ways of dealing with different
forms of the negative. However, many more instances in Russian occur to comply
with grammatical or traditional requirements, such as the negative form common
in questions or requests (see politeness formulas, page 72).

Conditionality – "what if …?"

Are we dealing with a hypothetical?

В случае если он не придет …
Suppose he doesn't come …

А что если придет?
What if he does?

(Будь я) на вашем месте, я бы …
If I were you, I would …

Ambiguity – not to panic!

Translators are often confronted with what looks like ambiguous wording in the
original text. They spend time and energy looking up potential solutions in the
dictionary whereas the answer is sometimes lurking in the text itself.

  For instance, participial phrases in Russian may be ambiguous, but the problem can be resolved in a number of ways:

  1. <u>Отдавая</u>, как всегда, должное моему собеседнику, я (все таки)
     заявляю, что он не прав.

With this type of concession, the participle should be relocated as a finite verb and/or changed to a subordinate or coordinate clause:

(Although) as always, I give my friend his due, I (still) say he's not right.
As ever, I give my friend his due, but I will say he is not right.
With all due respect, I must tell my friend that he is mistaken.

2. Вспоминая нашего друга, почтим (же) его память минутой молчания.

Here there is no indication of opposition, and the verb clearly indicates purpose, expressed through a participial phrase and a conjunction, "*as*," indicating time:

As we remember our friend, let us honor him with a moment of silence.

3. Отмечая заслуги оппонента, кандидат большую часть времени отвел на критику его «недостатков».
Although the candidate (*or give his name*) admitted that his opponent had his good points, he spent most of his time criticizing his "failures."

Or, in a variant allowing more scope for the imagination by not using "*although*" to spell out the concession function:

The candidate admitted that … , then spent most of his time …

The ambiguity in the participial phrase above is resolved in the context, which definitely points to a concession. Note also the concretization of отмечая to "*admitted*."

In the next example, the same word (Отмечая) and the same construction (participial) have a very different function, and this time there is no opposition:

4. Отмечая заслуги своего кандидата, оратор привел множество примеров его доброты и участия.
The speaker (*or his name*) called attention to many instances when the candidate's caring attitude found expression in his dealings with others.

Other kinds of ambiguity require some technical knowledge:

In Russian, дренажный сток could refer to a process or to the water involved. etc. So the translator must first clarify for himself what is meant, the process, a channel, or the runoff (liquid) itself, and only then decide on what the English should be.

A problem that is closer to home occurs in the next example:

Улицы города очистились от снега.

Consult the context to determine if the snow thawed or was removed. If there is a reference to when it happened, say, **рано**, then spring must have arrived early so the snow melted of its own accord. If on the other hand the street cleaners were particularly active, the answer would be that their efficiency did the trick. A problem in a non-technical text might not be so easily resolved:

> Она сшила себе платье **(сама или заказала?)**
> (*did she sew it herself or have it made to order?*)

> Она сделала (себе) прическу **(сама или в парикмахерской?)**
> (*herself or at the beauty salon?*)

Is it someone literally performing an action himself/herself, or requesting that the action be performed by someone else (to have something done, have someone do something for one …)? If an action in the original text is performed, caused, requested, or ordered, and the immediate context yields no information on that count, then the translator is in difficulty. Since the sentences above are ambiguous, their meaning needs to be elucidated in a broader context. Without a hint in the context as to who did the actual sewing or styling, etc., the question will remain unanswered: does this mean that "*she had a dress made (to order)*" and "*had her hair done at a salon*" or that "*she made herself a dress*" and "*did/styled her hair (herself)*"? There may be enough in the context to provide a clue, however, so don't give up too easily. In a similar case, the clue lies in the person's ability to perform a task, or whether he/she has the money to pay someone else to do it:

> Они построили (себе) дом на окраине.

This could be "*They built themselves a house on the edge of town*," but it probably isn't, not if the couple is too old, too sick, too busy, or too rich to do so themselves. The context might well provide that sort of information.

Another case where the context must be consulted to resolve a problem with ambiguity:

> Об этом ему говорить не надо: все это и так знают.

Should the translation be:

> It's not worth his talking about that because everyone knows it already.
> *or*
> It's *no good* / *no use* talking to him about that because everyone (including him) knows it already.

Here it is the ему that is causing the trouble, because without the context it is not clear whether advice is being offered regarding his talking about something, or others talking to him about it. What is the "*it*" that everybody knows already? Who is the "*he*," and is he capable of understanding the situation? If questions like that are answered in the context, it will surely come to the rescue!

Look to the context for explanation of puzzling homonyms (in this case, place names).

Теннис. Россиянки в Окланде.

Is that going to be "*Oakland, CA*" or "*Auckland, NZ*"? Scanning the context for clues, later in the item we see: "3 российские теннисистки выступили 1 января на турнире в Новой Зеландии." If the context had not given you such a clue, you could have consulted the Internet under "tennis tournaments, international" or "Russian tennis players." The end result:

Tennis. Russian women in Auckland
On January 1, three female players from Russia competed in a/the New Zealand tournament.

Note the concretization (specific verb for the general выступили.) Also remember that in English you cannot start a sentence with a number: it must either be spelled out or relocated in the translation. Lastly, whereas in the U.S. press, anyone living in Russia (except an expat) is routinely referred to as "a Russian," in Russia itself a distinction is made between the specifically ethnic русский and россиянин, who would be any citizen of Russia. This distinction also applies to the non-personal российская политика/ российские границы, etc.

Cognates – false friends and true enemies

"False friends" of the translator? Not really. Use cognates to your advantage. Just don't take them for granted.

Be on the lookout though for those ultra-friendly cognates, calques, and literalisms that seem to suggest an easy equivalent. They are not always wrong, as a matter of fact "*quality control*" is nearly a match for ОТК (отдел технического контроля), but every such "coincidence" deserves suspicion because they often are too good to be true, and some are downright dangerous.

A couple more relatively harmless examples:

реализовать свои возможности
realize one's potential

Это не комплимент. Я от всего сердца
That (compliment) wasn't just to please you. I really mean it.
I'm not just saying that (*to be nice / to make you feel good*).

However, if a hapless translator just put down the first cognate that came to mind, the result could well elicit a smile.

A cognate whose root is recognizably identical with a word in English might originate from a core idea (the etymology is obvious), but some have no discernable connection between the Russian and English "homonyms," regardless of etymology.

For example, актуальный is not "*actual*" but "*current*" or "*relevant*," as in:

его философия <u>актуальна</u> и сегодня
his philosophy is still <u>relevant</u> today

обсуждались <u>актуальные</u> вопросы
they examined <u>current</u> problems
they discussed the issues <u>of the day</u>

Or if the context warrants, even a contextual translation like "*important*" can be used.

More examples that often crop up in texts on various subjects are:

наблюдение и <u>контроль</u> на местах
onsite verification/monitoring

в том числе, его <u>капитальный</u> труд
including *a major study* / *a definitive work* / *his magnum opus*

Он знает множество <u>анекдотов</u>.
He knows lots/tons of funny stories.

Здесь скользко, ходите <u>аккуратно</u>!
(Be) careful! It's slippery here.
Watch out! The pavement is slick.

<u>формальный</u> подход
a perfunctory approach; superficial treatment

формальное отношение к делу
(just) going through the motions

Формально/Дается время подумать, на (самом) деле, требуют тут же отвечать.
Officially / *Technically* / *In theory*, you are given time to think, but actually you have to answer right away.

обслуживающий <u>персонал</u>
service <u>staff</u>; maintenance; repair <u>crew</u>; (*sometimes*) personnel

<u>кадры</u>
personnel; workers; staff (*not* cadres)
отдел <u>кадров</u>
department of human resources (*formerly:* personnel department)

кинокадры
film sequence; shot; take; scene; *individually:* frame

There is no singular in Russian corresponding to "*cadre*" (nucleus or activist group) in English. Humorously though, introducing your young child to colleagues at the workplace, someone could say:

Это—наш новый кадр? / Вот наш самый ценный кадр!
And this must be our newest *most valuable asset* / *member of our staff*!

Of a group of related words referring to "*getting rid of*" or "*putting an end to*" in English, some seem to boil down to "*liquidating*" in Russian:

<u>ликвидировать</u> пожар
put out / *extinguish* a fire (*with liquid, water, or any other way*)

<u>ликвидировать</u> последствия наводнений
deal with the flood damage (*to avoid a comic effect*)

<u>ликвидировать</u> задолженность
pay off a debt/mortgage

If we regard an "*organ*" as something that functions to serve its "parent" body, or some people would say, "*the greater good,*" then the following could be variations on that theme:

государственный <u>орган</u>
government agency (*or name the specific authority/body*)

<u>органы</u> печати / СМИ (средства массовой информации)
(print) media

Он работает в "органах."
(*an allusion to the secret service*)

Это <u>нормальный</u> процесс.
It is the usual/standard routine.

Как прошло заседание?   <u>Нормально.</u>
How did the meeting go?   All right.; As usual.; Pretty well.

Как себя чувствуете?   Нормально.
How do you feel?   All right.; Good.; Okay.; Fine.

реализация мечты
a dream come true

реализованные (с продажи) деньги/средства
money received from a sale

реализовать акции
sell shares/stock

реализовать преимущества системы
make use of the system's good points

реализовать планы
put plans into effect

реализовать ныне существующие возможности
take advantage of the available opportunities

More examples of automatic cognates that tend to crop up in translations:

Кому принадлежит приоритет?
Who was the first (to invent/achieve, etc.)? (*not*: priority)

пиетет перед (кем-то/чем-то)
(great) respect for (*not*: piety)

контролировать
monitor; supervise; regulate; watch (*usually not*: control)
(*Be extra careful of the cognate "control," making clear who is controlling whom.*)

адекватное поведение
rational/normal/appropriate behavior

неадекватная реакция
inappropriate/abnormal response; (*sometimes*) overreacting

санаторий
health resort; spa under medical supervision

Below are a few more examples, given with a translation and a misleading "automatic" version, to be avoided unless the context specifically calls for it:

моральный эффект
concerned with good and evil
not: moral effect
but: psychological effect

адекватный ответ
barely sufficient
not: adequate answer
but: acceptable/correct answer

авиация
if it is the science or practice of flying: aviation
but often: air fleet

на территории (страны/института/детского сада)
usually more specific: grounds; yard
rarely: territory
(*omit with* страны, *except in official documents*)

найти скрытые резервы
to unearth latent resources

Надо вызвать милицию!
Call the police/cops!

милиционер / участковый
precinct officer; (local) policeman; cop on the beat (*choose register as per context*)

военный объект
military installation; specifically: gun battery, camp, target

строительный объект
construction site

естественный объект
natural feature; *specifically*: mesa, river, lake, etc.

субъект (Федерации)
member of the (Russian) Federation

"Это еще тот субъект!"
"He's some type, all right!" (cf. "What a character!")
(*However, both* субъект *and* "*type*" *imply disapproval, and so are less likely to appear in a favorable context than* чудак *or* "*character.*")

Необходимо <u>выполнять</u> договоренности, <u>достигнутые</u> в Хельсинкском соглашении и за<u>фикс</u>ированные в Заключительном акте.
… <u>which</u> necessitates <u>honoring</u> commitments <u>under</u> the Helsinki Accords, in <u>conformity</u> with the Final Act.

This sentence is combined with the previous one in English. The translator dealt with the high-frequency verb выполнять and a potentially difficult past participle by changing it to a preposition, and also managed to avoid a cognate, *"fix."*

работники<u>, заинтересованные</u> в повышении выпуска продукции …
not: … who are interested in raising the output of production
but: … who have a stake in increasing output; … who have an
incentive to produce more

заинтересован does not mean интересуется (чем-то), which in a different context would be either *"take an interest in"* or *"wonder,"* as in:

Я интересуюсь этимологией.
I am interested in etymology.

Он интересовался, будешь ли ты завтра.
He was wondering/asking if you're going to be in tomorrow.

ведет к <u>активизации чего-то</u> …
… stimulates/promotes/speeds something up; stirs somebody to action;
brings something into play

Whether активизация is classed as an abstract or a process noun, the trouble is that in spite of its etymology, it slows down the "action" in this sentence, which would be "speeded up" if verbalized.

<u>По плану</u> <u>предусматривалось</u> <u>форсированное</u>/форсировать строительство.
The new plan called for *accelerated progress* on / *speeding up* construction
work.

A stereotypical start: A semi-operator followed by an impersonal reflexive form of the verb can be rendered using a noun in the nominative instead, coupled with an active verb; note also the potential cognate trap – we don't want to *"force"* anybody.

So with different contexts:

форсировать темпы строительства
if meant literally: speed (up) rate of construction work
if meant figuratively, also: quicken the pace of; make … a more rapid
advance to…; boost the development/accelerate (the economy);
rev up (progress)

Calques – "may I borrow that ...?"

Loan translations from another language are usually literalisms:

original expression	literal translation	recommended alternatives
особенность (стиля)	peculiarity	feature, distinction, overall character, fine point
дом отдыха	rest home	vacation hotel
(к <u>вопросу</u>) о чем-то (весь) <u>вопрос</u> в том, что	about the question of the whole question is	about, as to, in regard to smth in the fact that ...
<u>дело</u> в том, что ...	the matter is	the thing is; the trouble is; the fact is; the question is (*if there actually is a question, followed by, say*: ... a need to decide whether to do smth or not)

Закономерно is not generally connected with "*laws*" unless they are laws of nature or logic. Better options (as per context) would be:

predictably; was to be expected; that followed naturally/logically; that was in the course of events; in the order of things

Среди лидеров-<u>долгожителей</u> он стоит в первом ряду.
(A very old man), he has survived in office longer than most.
not: the long-lived leaders *or* long-standing leaders (*the reference to age depends on the context*)

серьезное <u>отставание</u> от современных норм
not: serious lag behind modern requirements
better: they have fallen far behind; they are not keeping pace with modern requirements; they are not keeping up with today's needs

в ра<u>счет</u>е на то, что ...
... reasoning that ...; expecting/hoping/figuring that ...
but also: ... the <u>calculation</u> being that ...; reckoning that ...

материальные ценности
not: material values
better: wealth, property, things

духовный
usually not: spiritual (*except in some contexts that do call for "spiritual"*)
better: inner; psychological

моральный
usually not: moral
better: emotional; inside

Физически было терпимо, а морально невыносимо.
Physically, it was tolerable; emotionally, it was unbearable.
Actually, it didn't hurt so much, but inside it really did.

By the way, don't forget that аморальный is not "*amoral*," which could characterize a person (or an animal) with no conception of right and wrong as we know it. The proper equivalent is "*immoral*":

аморальный поступок
immoral act

Syntax, Word Order, and the Message

The big problem facing the Russian-English translator is coping with two syntactic systems that are totally different. Failure to deal with the syntax effectively often leads to more than just an awkward English translation—it may be an out-and-out mistranslation. The main aim is to establish the author's intent behind his words and the order he has put them in.

Discovering function through syntax

How do you approach the important problem of the Russian word order? Look for the reason behind the structure to its function. Then starting with the function in the Russian sentence, translate the thought into English.

- Does the structure provide emphasis? Search out ways, lexical and/or syntactic, to find the answer.

- Is there a transition connecting a sentence with the previous one?

- Does it express a "theme-rheme" relation between the setting (<u>background,</u> or <u>topic</u>) and the point being made (the <u>nub</u>, the raison d'être of the sentence)?

The syntax of the two Russian sentences below provides a clue to the question the translator could ask himself in order to pinpoint the function of the original sentence and produce an accurate and effective translation.

Мы с Сашей пошли <u>в кино</u>.
Sasha and I went <u>to the movies</u>.

Question: What did you do? (*the answer is in the entire sentence*)
    or
    Where did you and Sasha go? (<u>в кино</u> *in the important final position*)

Я пошла в <u>кино</u> с <u>Сашей</u>.
I <u>went to the movies</u> with <u>Sasha</u>.

Question: What did you do? (*the first half of the sentence, up to* "с <u>Сашей</u>")
    or
    Whom did you go with? (с <u>Сашей</u>)

One way to emphasize a key word is by giving it preferred placement in the sentence, often at the end, but sometimes where there would naturally be a voice stress.

Word order in Russian only appears to be freer and less rigid than in English. But since Russian has its own rules, be aware that the word order in the original text contains clues as to what the author considered key. In addition, the siting of words in the sentence implies a certain intonation. Or a sentence may have been structured so that the author's thought could flow easily through the text as a whole. In building your English sentence, be sure to reflect the intention of the author as you see it. Note that if the original text were to be read aloud, the intonation would be governed by the meaning inherent in the context. The context will prompt your syntactic choice according to the sense.

Где вы были?
Where were you? (*non-emotive, no particular "voice" stress; this is simply a request for information*)

cf: Где вы бывали/побывали/были?
Where/What (interesting) places have you *been to / traveled to / visited*? (*non-emotive*)

Где вы (такие-сякие) <u>были</u>?
Where (on earth) have you <u>been</u>? (*highly emotive, implies concern, worry, possibly anger*)

А где были <u>вы</u>?
Where were <u>you</u>? (*as opposed to someone else, non-emotive*)

А <u>вы</u>-то были где?
(Well,) Where were <u>you</u> then? (*not someone else, emotive*)

Вы были <u>где</u>?

You were <u>where</u>? (*request for a repeat, non-emotive; or surprise or disbelief, emotive as per context*)

Context – its crucial importance

In coping with any questions concerning the original text and your translation, including those about repetition and ambiguous formulations in Russian, a primary source of help is the context. The logic or a clue found there can be vital. Only then will dictionaries come into the picture. This cannot be stressed too often.

For word choice
• put across the sense, and not a wrong or misleading sense
• repeat or not, perhaps using a synonym or pro-form
• insert or omit words
• conform to the proper style level
• try a complete makeover/total transformation—do not translate separate words
• change parts of speech—just try to provide the overall sense

For syntax (clarity, proper emphasis, smooth and easy reading, and/or greater effect)
• siting of key words
• providing end weight for balance
• clarifying the theme-rheme relationship
• choosing active, passive, "pseudo-active," or another verb form
• introducing "fillers," including extra synonyms

But most important of all, context will help determine the intended meaning and tone, often resolving ambiguity.

Polysemantic and high-frequency units
The problems with such words are meaning and "valence" (combinability—"what goes with what?"). Polysemantic words, those that in different contexts have different meanings, fall into several categories. Make sure you understand the Russian text. Some of these words are just homonyms, with distinctly different meanings, even though there may be some real or fancied connection between them, such as shape. Take *коса,* which can be translated *scythe, braid,* or *spit/sand bar,* depending on the context. Such words should not pose any particular difficulty for a translator who pays context the attention it is due.

Other words are clearly grouped around a central idea, in a common semantic field. While their meanings do not differ radically, for clarity's sake they require a connection to the right "partners" with which they could be paired. Examples, with partners, include:

Бетховен посвятил свое произведение Элизе.
Beethoven dedicated this piece to Elise.

Вавилов посвятил свою жизнь служению науке.
Vavilov devoted his (entire) life to science.

Пришлось посвятить целый день выяснению причины.
I would devote all day *trying to find / looking for* the reason.

In the third example, depending on the larger context, пришлось посвятить is emotionally loaded, referring to a degree of frustration, etc., because in a more objective setting, the verb would probably have been потратил.

Remember, ambiguity involving polysemantic problems can be resolved by consulting the context. Below are a few examples, with "partners" as mini-context:

завышенные нормы
too high (*possibly unattainable, such as*: "goals set too high")

завышенные данные
too high; exaggerated (*whether it is performance figures or other data, deliberately doctored or not*)

лицо

лицо (человек)	individual, person, people, anyone
официальное лицо	official (*noun*)
духовное лицо	cleric, clergyman, priest, minister, pastor (*specific per context*)
лицо / образ / личность	personality, image
лицо нашего журнала	the image/face/look of our magazine

культура

культура рабочего места	a well-organized workplace
режиссерская культура	a (theatrical) director's craft; standards; ethic (*as per context*)
вести себя культурно	behave (oneself); be civilized; mind one's manners (*as per context*)

Even when the meaning in the Russian is clear, it is important to look for accepted collocations in English:

очередное учебное плавание
routine training voyage

При очередной задержке нажимайте/нажмите вот эту кнопку.
Every / *The next* time it stops, just push this button.

Вам удобно в этом кресле?
Are you comfortable/okay in that chair?

Удобно ли будет просить ...?
Would it be all right to ask for ...?

Как-то неудобно ...
It doesn't seem very nice ... / I'd be embarrassed ...

всем удобное решение/решение, удобное для всех
mutually advantageous; everyone was easy/comfortable with that
   (solution/decision)

стимулировать поощрять (кого ... на что)
способствовать (чему) ... подталкивать на (что)
encourage, push, urge, spur (someone ... to do something)

налоговые стимулы
tax breaks/incentives

Тогда стимулировались и затем разворачивались "территориальные
   комплексы" (Khrushchev-era economics).
Development of the "territorial complexes" was at/in the initial stage(s).
Work on (implementing) the "territorial complexes" was only getting started.
(*Note: quotation marks for first mention only*)

руководящие органы	executive bodies
руководящие кадры	executives, managers
руководство	the management (*people*); management (*process*)
руководство	(printed) (user) manual
растущее недовольство	mounting anger, resentment (*because "displeasure" would be too weak for the given context*)

Ты когда-нибудь будешь доволен?
Are you ever/never going to be satisfied?
Will nothing ever please you?

Его ожидает множество проблем/испытаний на новом поприще
He faces many challenges in this/his new *field of activity / profession / job.*

More polysemantic problems with solutions:

снять In addition to "*take off,*" there are many related translations:

снять боль	relieve (the) pain
снять вопрос	drop/remove an item (from the agenda)
снять свою кандидатуру	withdraw (from the race); drop out
снять усталость	refresh; make one feel like new

Это средство как рукой <u>сняло усталость</u>.
The remedy worked like a charm—my fatigue was completely gone.

With strict attention to context, besides, of course, prepositions and case endings, a look-alike won't waylay you. Otherwise … watch your step:

художественный

художественная литература	literature, belles lettres, fiction
художественная школа	art school (educational)
but:	
школа/направление в искусстве	school, movement in art (trend/style)
художественная гимнастика	(rhythmic) gymnastics
художественный фильм	movie, (feature) film (*not*: art film)

большой

большой спорт	big-time sports
большое искусство	real art; the world of art

лицо

На лице у нее выступил яркий румянец.
She *blushed / turned beet red.*

На лице у него остались «результаты» драки.
The results of the brawl were *on his face / plain to see.*

осваивать (cf. усваивать, which also means "*to learn/understand/internalize*," but in a different context or combination "*to learn a lesson; to understand a principle*")

осваивать новый вид продукции	develop a new line (of products)
осваивать технику	(learn to) use (*depending on Russian aspect*)
осваивать метод (работы)	master
осваивать ресурсы	tap, utilize

осваивать производство (чего-либо) (сейчас осваивают *or* уже освоили ...)
(learn to) produce (*or depending on Russian aspect*)

осваивать новые производственные мощности
start up, commission (facilities, plants)

объем

объем бака/емкости
capacity, volume (of a tank/container)

объем текста	length; size; pages
объем работ	amount; range; span

объем работ в эти дни настолько велик, что ...
There is so much *to do / to be done / that needs doing.*
So much needs to be done that ...

эксплуатация In addition to the core meaning of "*exploitation*" other options are:

эксплуатация детского труда	child labor
эксплуатация машины	operating/running a machine/car, etc.

быт (day-to-day/ordinary) life

заедает быт	the daily routine takes up too much time
	I have no time for anything but my chores
бытовое обслуживание	personal/consumer services
	or specifically: laundry, barber's, shoe repair, etc.
бытовая техника	household appliances

выступать Besides the core meaning of *"coming out"* or *"making oneself visible"* (for some purpose), other options are:

выступать (перед ...) (с речью)
speak to, address (an audience), make a speech

выступать на сцене / на (спортивной) арене и т.п.
perform/appear (on stage); play, compete

выступать за/против
be for/against; come out *in favor of / against* (something); speak *in favor of / against* (something)

ставить In addition to *"set"* or *"stand,"* ставить can be used in many different collocations:

ставить своей целью	aim to (do something)
ставить голос	train the voice
ставить балет	choreograph a ballet
ставить спектакль	stage a play/opera
ставить на карту	bet, stake, risk
ставить на голосование	put to the vote

ставить вопрос о выводе его из (состава) комитета
raise/broach the question/possibility of *removing him from the committee / getting him to resign*

ставить(себя) под удар
jeopardize; threaten; put in harm's way; stick one's neck out

охрана One translation for this noun is *"protection,"* but there is also:

охрана детства	child welfare
охрана природы	wildlife management; environmental protection; nature conservation
охрана	security; bodyguards (in a building, of a person/ delegation)

средства Besides *"the means (to do something),"* other translations are:

средства массовой информации (СМИ)
the media

средство от головной боли
headache remedy

не хватает средств
not to have the funds; be overdrawn; be short (of an amount of money)

средство передвижения
vehicle, conveyance, carrier, transport

направление In addition to the primary meaning of направление "*direction* (*to*/ *from*)" there is:

направление к врачу	referral to a specialist/doctor
направление	school, movement (in art), *cf.* art school
направление	line (of research); area of study (in science)
направление поиска	line of inquiry

памятник All the terms using памятники listed below have something in common with one another, but because of the narrow application of the primary meaning, "*in memory*," they can rarely be translated as "*gravestone*" or "*memorial*" and depend entirely on the context for meaning and translation. This might range from "*book*" to "*statue*" to "*cathedral*."

памятник (кому-то) памятники культуры
statue of somebody; monument to somebody; cultural treasure; the sights; the classics (*generalized*); buildings; architecture; painting; sculpture (*or specific examples*)

памятники архитектуры
the notable architecture (of a town); examples (of architecture) of a particular era; specific important buildings/palaces/churches

памятники литературы
literary landmarks; the classics

памятники письменности
ancient manuscripts/inscriptions

создавать Can be translated as "*make*" or "*create*" but preferably should be more concrete, for instance answering the question "*what goes with what?*"— something only the context can answer:

Они обещали создать все условия.
They said they would <u>provide</u> the right/necessary conditions.

Корпорация создана в 1917 году.
The corporation was <u>founded</u> in 1917.

Нужно подумать о создании филиала.
We ought to *think* / *be thinking* about <u>opening</u> a *branch office / subsidiary*.

создавать полотна
… to <u>paint</u> (pictures)

создавать музыку
… to <u>compose/write</u> (music)

Я хочу <u>творить</u>! Создавать подлинные произведения искусства!
I want to create (real art)!

These last two examples project lofty, perhaps youthful, ambitions similar to (but not age-related) to мое творчество, which hopefully will not be translated as "*my art*," unless you detect some irony in the author's intention. This combination comes across as tone deaf in both languages, so a better solution would be "*my work*," or specifically, "*my painting*," "*my music*," "*my movies*," etc.

творчество This related word has some of the same challenges:

жизнь и творчество <u>замечательного</u> артиста (имярек)
The life and work of (the <u>distinguished/remarkable/outstanding</u>) actor (*or give name*).

But please, don't use "*wonderful*." Better omit the epithet altogether, because if he had been all that terrific, none of this praise would be necessary today. Besides, television viewers in the U.S. are probably inured to advertisers claiming the most extraordinary advantages for their products, so an extra "*wonderful*" in our translation might fail to impress. This advice would not apply to personal, as compared with professional qualities:

<u>Творчество</u> Дюрера <u>сохранила</u> свою свежесть сквозь века.
Durer's paintings have not lost their freshness of centuries ago.
Durer's paintings are as fresh as they once were centuries ago.

Here are two good solutions in one sentence: specific instead of general, and an antonymic translation besides.

А <u>творчество</u> гроссмейстера <u>поучительно</u> уже потому, что он чувствовал гармонию фигур.
<u>To study</u> *his / the grandmaster's* <u>game/thinking</u> is instructive/worthwhile if only because it demonstrates a real understanding of the harmony between the pieces.

Note the way the syntax is juggled around for a clear and smooth presentation, also the contextual, concretized treatment of the "*creativity*."

These further examples demonstrate flexibility in conveying the essence of polysemantic words in various contexts. The idea is not to be stuck with one "all-purpose" solution.

развертывать (деятельность)	go into action; launch (a project) (*if the context tells you that you need something more specific*)
развернуть ракеты по всему фронту	deploy/site missiles over the entire frontline
развернутое объяснение	detailed explanation
отражать общие цели	point to common goals
формальный подход	a perfunctory approach; superficial treatment
формальное отношение к делу	(just) going through the motions
формально / в принципе	theoretically

Формально/По идее, можно не декларировать доходы, **полученные** из другой страны, но зато теряются лишние "кварталы," необходимые для **получения** государственной пенсии.
Officially / Technically / In theory, you are not required to declare income from abroad, but if you take advantage of that option, you stand to lose calendar quarters when you have earned at least the minimum, making you eligible for Social Security benefits in the future.

В принципе, рукопись уже готова, только надо подчистить одну главу.
The manuscript is finished, to all intents and purposes. There is only one chapter I need to *go over / clean up*.

становление (государства)
establishment, formation, rise; *can also be used as a finite verb, e.g.*: come into being

становление льда
ice formation; the ice cover

роль
part (played); function; place; job; responsibility

"Какова его роль в этом деле?"
"What was so-and-so's role/part?"
"What did so-and-so (actually) do?"

принимать участие In addition to the old faithfuls: *"participate"* and *"take part,"* don't be afraid of contextual or specific solutions, e.g.:

(активно) участвовать
get/be involved in; be into (an activity) (*if the context will tolerate an informal translation*)

участвовать в игре/турнире
play (in) a game; compete in a tournament

принимать (посильное)
volunteer (in a specific project); be a part of ...; do what one can for ...

участники (конференции)
conferees; those at the conference; those attending; attendees
specifically: bankers, lawmakers, etc. (*according to the context*)

светлый
fine, serene (person/character); happy (time); bright

светлая грусть   bittersweet, melancholy; mixed feelings

светлая комната/квартира   sunny; sun-filled (rooms)

Светлые корпуса придают свежий вид всему району.
The bright new (exterior) brick imparts a fresh vibrant new look.
The light-colored brick gives the neighborhood a fresh vibrant new look.

волнение
emotion; excitement; anxiety; worry; strong/emotional feeling; stage fright; thrill (*for example, upon seeing the Statue of Liberty for the first time*)

волнующий
exciting, emotional

вопрос, сейчас волнующий нас
the issue/problem/thing that *concerns us / is worrying us / is very much on our minds* today ... (*see context for clues*)

Она страшно волнуется
She is terribly nervous (anxious)/excited (exhilarated) (*see context for clues*)
but:
нервничает   ... is anxious/worried
however:
Он человек нервный.   He's a nervous person. (*habitually*)
                              He has a problem with nerves.

принимать (Possibly omit where a verbalized variant is available and appropriate.):

принимать меры	act, take measures
принимать законы	legislate, pass/enact/make laws
принимать гостей	entertain, have people/friends over
принимать решение	decide, make a decision
принимать участие	participate, take part

More polysemantic words with "partners":

воспитанник преподавателя/маэстро
pupil

воспитанник института
student; graduate, alumnus (of a college)

воспитанник российской школы (<u>пианистики</u>)
a product of the Russian *piano school / school of piano playing*

воспитанник/стипендиат
protégé (*contextual near synonym*); supported by an institution/foundation (*verbalized*); grantee (*for a quasi-legal document*)

High-frequency units

общественная жизнь
community life/activities (*remember that "social life" could also mean just "socializing"*)

общественный деятель
community activist; civic/community leader; public figure (*only if not contrasted/compared with "politician," as in*: политические и общественные деятели). *Or else a more specific word should be used in place of "public figure," not always feasible, as politicians are public figures, too* [*see below*]: advocate for some cause; philanthropist; *but "public figure" can be used when accompanied by an indication of the type of activity, specifically*: "community leader," "human rights activist," "philanthropist."

государственные и общественные деятели
statesmen; political/civic leaders; politicians; community activists

на общественных началах/общественная работа
on a volunteer basis; pro bono; unpaid/community/volunteer work
not: voluntary *or* public

общественник
community activist; volunteer

меры общественного воздействия
or
Общественность контролирует деятельность (официальных лиц)
public oversight; community impact; (measures involving) pressure by the
  community
(*A careless translation might suggest "control of the public," rather than
"control by the public." The question the translator has to keep in mind is
"who is controlling whom?"*)

Other high-frequency words and phrases

This category includes prop words—how to recognize them and what to do about
them so as not to clutter up a translation needlessly. Since the words and phrases
in the following list are in such constant use in Russian writing, at least in certain
categories of writing, the Russian reader knows when they can be ignored. He
can also guess the meaning. The reader of the translation has no such advantage
so the translator must try out different variants to see if the ineffectual prop word
can be eliminated. But there are other words and collocations that occur all too
frequently, or so it seems to us translators—and, unfortunately, the readers too if
the translator does not recognize the irritant for what it is and make an effort to
remedy the situation.

Translators stand to gain little from always using the same English equivalent
for a frequently occurring Russian word in text after text. Taking a few minutes
to search out a substitute is worth it. If the translated text is repetitive, dull, or
unconvincing, we—and of course, the author—are likely to lose our readers.

**Some alternative word choices for tired old, automatic ("generic") transla-
tions** (though the older equivalents could conceivably be pressed into service
one more time):

Russian	Generic	Alternatives
достижения / успехи	achievements, successes	(past) performance, (track) record
проблема	problem, difficulty	challenge, issue, concern
раздражение	irritation	*noun*: displeasure, anger *verb*: frown upon
задача	task	job, business, mission, objective
противоречие	contradiction	conflict, paradox; absurdity (*as per context*)

противоречивый	contradictory	inconsistent, conflicting (*as per context*)
сложный	complex	difficult (character); intricate (workings); far from simple
позитивные сдвиги	positive movement	(some) progress

Consider a word that is often taken for granted by the translator: особенность should not be translated as the noun "*peculiarity*" except when it means "*strangeness*," because that notion will step in unwonted anyway. The sense seems clear enough when one sees the word in context, but even the hard-working "*feature*," which one finds in so many English original texts, cannot be made to fit every Russian text that contains особенность, especially in high-frequency combinations, like "особенность этой теории в том, что ..." and "особенностью нового метода является то, что ...". Try a specific contextual solution, say: "*the advantage/virtue/beauty of the new method is the speed with which ...*" But if such a translation does not seem warranted, then perhaps a more general solution is required: "*one thing about ...*" or even "*a feature peculiar to ...*" would be acceptable. In addition to "*(distinctive) feature*" an expanded, but stylistically less formal solution might be "*what makes it different is ...*". So, unless it is clear that the author disapproves of that particular "feature," do not use "*peculiarity*."

High frequency units with effective translations:

дискуссия <u>вокруг</u> / <u>по поводу</u> (мер доверия) / о мерах доверия
talks <u>concerning</u>/<u>on</u> confidence-building measures

прием

(прием вторсырья/посуды)	recycling center
(прием посетителей)	visiting hours (sign)
(прием гостей)	entertaining (friends, etc.)
(пышный прием)	elaborate reception

он прекрасный <u>специалист</u> (в области кардиологии, и т.п.)
preferably not: ... a wonderful/excellent specialist
better to be specific: a good/excellent heart (*or other area*) specialist/doctor; an excellent cardiologist/ophthalmologist/engineer/ editor, etc.

(настоящий) спец / умелец / прекрасно разбирается в ... / "дока"
a real pro; *or be specific*: a real pro with computers, etc. (*usually referring to a skilled amateur*); very good at ... (*generalization*); is an expert, is a real pro

новый <u>курс</u> внешней политики	a new foreign policy
держать <u>курс</u> на ...	strive/work for
Держите меня в курсе.	Keep in touch.
Не падайте духом! Держитесь!	Don't give up!, Don't despair!, Don't be discouraged!, Hang in there!

But if worse comes to worst:

| Так держать! | Stay the course! |

Среди весьма вероятных нововведений – <u>создание</u> на луне крупных <u>объектов</u> обслуживаемых людьми.
Among the projects *likely to be considered / that have a good chance* are manned industrial/research centers on the moon.
(*Note the use of* создание *as a prop in the Russian, expendable in the translation. Also* объект *is made more specific, to fit the context.*)

А большая часть населения, <u>воспитана</u> на стереотипах мышления, не готова к новому подходу.
Yet a significant part of the population, <u>conditioned</u> by *stereotypes / standardized ways of thinking* is not yet ready for *a new approach / anything new.*
or
Yet a significant part of the population who grew up (literally) <u>surrounded</u> by stereotypes is not yet ready for *a new approach / anything new.*

EMPHASIS AND DE-EMPHASIS

In emphasizing or de-emphasizing a word, phrase or sentence to make it correspond to the semantic load it has in the original Russian, it is important to establish what the author really means, and act accordingly. Techniques of pointing up or playing down an element in the sentence can help to highlight and bring out the thought more effectively. Emphasis in a Russian sentence should be considered from several angles before deciding on how emphatic or expressive to make that sentence or a component in English. The author's intention should be our main concern: maybe he did not mean something quite so dramatic. What degree of emphasis could he have had in mind, as compared to what he actually said, since there is often a difference. Or perhaps there are already many emphatic or expressive words in the immediate vicinity. Then again it may be that the syntax already provides emphasis. How to decide? Weighing the word in question in the larger context should be of immediate help. In the long term, however, experience with other people's texts on a related subject, with translations, is truly invaluable.

Intensifiers (amplifiers)

An intensifier adds to the impact of the word it modifies, though it is occasionally employed for balance. Try to establish the intention of the author (possibly from the context), then either use an intensifier or substitute a stronger single <u>referential</u> word without an intensifier, but only if needed.

> Он <u>снова</u> и нудно <u>перечислял весь</u> список своих бед.
> Then he <u>would go right back</u> to his <u>litany</u> of ills.

Here the intensifier is omitted, substituted for by a stronger key word. Note the imperfective aspect, rendered in English by the whole modal phrase, expressing habitual action.

In the next examples an extra synonym and inversion are used in Russian, repetition in English:

> Надо работать, трудиться надо!
> You must work, and work hard!

> Наше дело <u>правое</u>. Мы на <u>верном</u> пути.
> Our <u>cause</u> is a good <u>cause</u>. We are on the right track.

Repetition tends to emphasize the thought: compare with *"our cause is good"* or *"our cause is a good one,"* which is not nearly as effective.

You will have to decide whether a Russian modifier is an intensifier or not. Does it have an essential meaning of its own or does it only serve to amplify (perhaps needlessly in English) the meaning of the word it modifies?

1. If the modifier is an intensifier and must be retained to preserve the intended meaning, there may be an existing accepted collocation in English:

   > Это явно так, бросается в глаза!
   > It's so obvious, even *an idiot / a blind man* can see it.
   > (*if warranted by the context*)

2. If the modifier is an intensifier and you are considering leaving it out, see if the word modified by the intensifier in the Russian can be replaced by a single, but stronger, more expressive word in English (here, an "adverbial verb") because an unmodified, unadorned word, which sometimes has more force than one with a modifier, would make the intensifier superfluous:

Машина с грохотом пронеслась по улице.
or
проехала на большой скорости.
The car roared up the street.
The car sped/streaked by.

3. If you conclude that the force of the Russian word should be retained, don't forget to choose carefully among the different English adjective/adverb forms.

4. If the Russian intensifier would only serve to clutter up your sentence, see if you can safely omit it, as long as it does not substantially change the import.

5. If it is necessary to emphasize a point, or even to liven up an entire text, you can make good use of such colloquial expressions as "body words" or other humanizing tactics.

Мы ждем, а он все тянет.
We wait and wait, but he's still dragging his feet.

Да что вы говорите!
You don't say!

Recognizing the emphasis in the Russian is half the battle. Finding adequate expression in English will take care of the rest:

Various parts of speech can be used for emphasis:

(Собственно/Именно/А) этого и добивался режим в качестве опоры.
And that is <u>just</u> the kind of support the regime had been seeking.

Где <u>же</u> все это?
(So) where is all that? (*or underline or italicize the "is"*)

Взять <u>хотя бы</u> такой случай ...
Take something like this ...; A good example ...

... <u>ярко</u> показал <u>всю</u> безнадежность положения.
... demonstrated/exposed/showed (up) *the hopelessness of the situation / how absolutely hopeless it was.*
(*Note the shifted epithet, helping to put across the emphasis felt in the original.*)

<u>Уже</u> в следующем году будет готово.
It will be ready/finished *as early as / no later than* next year.

Уже и в мирное время не было послабления.
Even in peacetime there was no letup.

Уже через год начались ссоры.
In (just) another year they began fighting (again).
or omit the intensifier:
One year later, they began fighting (again).

А безобразия продолжались вплоть до следующего года.
The disgraceful state of affairs continued (right) *up to / into* the following year.

... заведомо/наперед (*colloq.*) знал
Knowing that ...; He knew it all the time ...; He knew it full well ...;
  He knew it perfectly well ...; He was well aware ...; It was premeditated;
  He did smth with aforethought/deliberately

заведомая ложь
a deliberate/barefaced lie

Является ни чем иным как признание своей беспомощности.
That was an admission that he was utterly helpless.
(*The shifted epithet helps put the idea across, rather than just translating the*
  words.)

суровое испытание
a bitter/cruel/harsh trial

Свято чтим память павших.
We *always honor* / *hold dear* the memory of the fallen.
The memory of the fallen is sacred (to/for us).
We will always remember the fallen.

А он свято верит этой ерунде. / А он свято верит в такую ерунду.
He is foolish enough to believe such nonsense.
And he actually believes that stuff.
He is utterly sure that it's for real.
(*Version three above is effective if the context makes clear the ironical intent.*
  Watch out for irony that might "steal the identity" of a perfectly respectable
  word; свято here is used only as an intensifier, albeit a roguish one.)

Они и не думают выводить свои войска.
They have (absolutely) no plans to withdraw (their troops).
(*This is another case of a transferred epithet, lending strength to the entire*
  sentence.)

основа основ
cornerstone; sine qua non; the very foundation of

Я часто-часто думаю о тебе.
I'm <u>always</u> thinking of you.
I <u>never stop</u> thinking about you. (*antonymic translation*)

Мероприятие проведено <u>успешно.</u>
The event went off smoothly.

Это <u>еще</u> можно понять.
That much *can be understood / is understandable*.
That could be explained.
One could find some sort of an explanation for that.

Решение вызвало <u>гневный</u> протест …
People are angry over the decision to …
People have voiced anger over the decision to …
Angry protests greeted the decision.
The decision has aroused/elicited/provoked nothing but anger.
The decision met with angry protests from …
(*Only the last two versions above retain the form of the original; the first two are examples of the conversive tactic.*)

Я всю (оставшуюся) жизнь буду хранить эту память.
I will (always) <u>treasure</u> this memory.
(*Or add "forever" or "to the end of my life" for end weight and to preserve the emotional charge of the intensifier in the original.*)

Эту реликвию мы у себя <u>бережно</u> храним.
It is a treasured heirloom.
(*Or add "for us" at the beginning, or "in this family" at the end; either one will contribute to the rhythmic flow of the English sentence and preserve the emotional charge of the intensifier in the Russian.*)

Полотна <u>бережно</u> хранили в течение <u>всей</u> блокады Ленинграда.
The paintings were <u>watched over</u> and <u>kept safe</u> throughout the siege.
(*The two seemingly unemotional phrases combine to make the sentence above flow and, once again, preserve the emotion of the original, eliminating the need for the two intensifiers, "carefully" and "entire."*)

Мы стараемся к нему <u>бережно</u> относиться, а то ведь ему уже столько пришлось пережить.
We try to spare him. He has gone through so much already.

Начальника полюбили из-за его <u>бережного</u> отношения к подчиненным.
The boss earned the affection of his employees by his <u>caring</u> and <u>respectful</u> attitude to them.
(*another illustration of the conversive tactic*)

Будем <u>неукоснительно</u> следовать его принципиальной политике.
We will <u>closely</u> follow his principled policies.
We will always *be loyal / hold <u>fast</u> / adhere <u>strictly</u>* to his principled policies.

Прошло <u>ровно</u> 20 лет с тех пор, как ...
It has been 20 years <u>to the day</u> that ...

<u>Много</u> лет спустя ...
Years later...; It was not until years later that ...
(The intensifier is omitted for dramatic effect.)

<u>Сделали всего</u> за <u>несколько</u> минут ...
It took just minutes.
(The conversive tactic is used here again, plus one intensifier omitted for
  dramatic effect; cf. the tamer version: "(just) a few minutes.")

Через <u>всего лишь</u> несколько секунд ...
(<u>Just</u>) Seconds later, ...
(Here the intensifier can be retained or omitted without loss of meaning.)

Он опоздал <u>всего (лишь)</u> на несколько минут.
He was <u>only</u> a few minutes late.
(In this example, the intensifier should be retained as it could influence
  further developments in the tardy gentleman's life.)

У них (есть) много-много игрушек.
They have *lots (and lots)/tons of* toys.

<u>грубое</u> вмешательство
(gross) interference; (<u>outrageous</u>) meddling
(In version 2 here the intensifier can be omitted because the noun is already
  emotionally loaded; cf. the more neutral "intervention.")

Он <u>менее всего</u> был склонен подчиняться такому приказу.
He was <u>not at all</u> inclined to obey an order like that.
He had <u>no intention</u> of obeying such an order.

<u>чрезвычайно</u> важный момент
a <u>crucial</u> consideration/factor/aspect
(Intensifier omitted, replaced by a stronger modifier. Note: a careful trans-
lator has avoided a mistaken rendition of момент *as an English look-alike*
[cognate])

А <u>ведь</u> / <u>как известно</u>, там, где (есть) А, <u>обязательно </u>будет и Б.
Of course, / *Well,* where there is an "x," there is <u>bound to</u> be a "y."

придает <u>определенное</u> своеобразие
gives/lends it a quality/spirit/character/flavor <u>all its own</u>
(*cf. "a certain spirit," etc. which would be too bland; note also the valuable final position of "all its own."*)

Сдержит ли он свое слово?
Will he keep his word (though)?

>   <u>Несомненно</u>/ <u>без всякого сомнения</u>/ <u>обязательно</u> сдержит.
>   *not*: He doubtless will. (*actually implies some doubt*)
>   *but*: Undoubtedly. (*a more assured answer*)
>   *or*: No doubt about it.; Beyond a doubt. (*even better*)
>   *or*: Absolutely. (*the best option here*)

… <u>с (единственной) целью</u> его опередить
… with the <u>sole</u> purpose of getting there first
… with the idea of <u>beating him to it</u>
(*Version 1 does translate the intensifier, but version 2 transfers the emphasis to an attention-grabbing expression instead.*)

для пущей важности / ради понта
(just) to look (more) important; to put on the dog; to show off
(*Emphasis in the English is achieved through a transferred epithet or an added intensifier.*)

Some mild intensifiers allow several options:

(целый) ряд
a number of; numerous; many; quite a few

несколько
When used as an adjective, and the context is not neutral, watch out for "*a few*," which will limit your options; better: "*some*," "*several*," "*a number of*," or simply use the plural of the noun modified. The other meaning of несколько comes into play when it is used as an adverb, meaning "*somewhat*," another ploy of the cautious writer of scholarly texts.

весьма
This word does not always need to be translated as an intensifier in English, but can possibly be rendered as "*quite*" or "*very*," but in any case, <u>not</u> "*rather*."

достаточно
This does not always mean "*enough*," "*sufficiently*," or "*adequately*"; though much used by scholars in need of verbal "insurance," it can often be

omitted. When it is an essential element of the thought, it can be retained, perhaps as a mild intensifier:

> К тому времени стало достаточно ясно, что они никуда не уедут.
> By that time it was (pretty/fairly) clear that they would not be going anywhere.

Extra words (or fewer words) for emphasis:

> Tourist: "Вы закрыли столовую на обед?!"
>   "You <u>actually</u> closed the cafeteria for lunch!"

> Busboy: "А мы что, не люди?"
>   "Well, we're human, too, <u>if you want to know.</u>"

The punctuation in the original (to express outrage) is compensated for by the intensifier in the translation, while the offended tone of the explanation, including the rhetorical question in the original, is expressed through the addition of a snippy reply in the translation, which also serves to balance out the sentence.

Sometimes a conscious decrease in emphatic words will have a stronger effect in the English text. Take the following sentence as an example:

> Он <u>безапелляционно декларирует</u>, что <u>будто</u> сорвал встречу я.

Depending on the tone of the context, the translation might go (in descending order of emphasis) from "overwrought" to "on target":

> He has the <u>gall</u> to <u>allege</u> that I was the <u>culprit</u> who threw a <u>monkey wrench</u> into the works.
> (*The surfeit of strong words and expressions actually weakens the effect of the sentence, making it almost comical and definitely unconvincing.*)

> He states in the <u>most peremptory</u> tone that it was I who <u>sabotaged</u> the talks.
> (*This is closer to the desired effect, as long as the context does not have enough expressive words already.*)

> <u>Now it *seems / turns out*</u> that <u>I</u> caused the talks to collapse.
> (*Ironical understatement is often more effective than "faithful" overstatement.*)

> He <u>is claiming</u> it was I who disrupted the talks.
> (*If the context requires a calmer, more objective tone, the continuous [progressive] form of the verb still supplies some emphasis.*)

An additional synonym is occasionally (but stereotypically) used for balance in the Russian, or just by inertia. Sometimes the author is not satisfied with the emphasis in his sentence and has called in reinforcements. Try translating that additional unit, then make your own judgment as to whether it is necessary in English.

Его жизнь и судьба необычны.
His (life) *was / has been* an extraordinary one/life.
He *led / has led / had* an extraordinary life.

Автор сценария вложил много своего, личного.
The author of the screenplay put something of his own into it.
His personality/philosophy *is evident throughout / shines through on every page.*

When intensifiers need to be omitted, they are sometimes compensated for by the use of an expressive verb or another word:

Реализация этого плана влечет за собой самые гибельные последствия.

1. This plan is fraught with dangerous consequences ...
   (*the emotive "fraught" compensates for the omission of* "самые")
2. ... with what may be disastrous results ...
3. ... with what could only be total disaster ...
4. ... and there is no telling what the consequences might be.
   (*a dark hint + the modal word lends an emotional, personal touch*)
5. ... and there is no telling what harm it could do.
6. This plan will lead to total disaster.
7. This plan will surely lead to disaster.
8. This plan can only lead to disaster.
9. *Or OMIT the intensifier* самые *with or without compensation;*
   гибельные *by itself is bad enough.*

самых разнообразных форм
in a (great) variety of shape; in all (sorts of) shapes; in every shape and form

... допустил грубейший промах/прокол.
... made a (colossal/real) blunder.

Use a stronger, more expressive word, with or without an intensifying adjective, or transform "промах" into a verb, adjusting the syntax:

He bungled his response.
He botched the operation.

Adverbial units as intensifiers:

Надо только настоять на своем и мы конечно (же) справимся с оппозицией.
If we *persist / stick to our guns*, we could (definitely) overcome all opposition.
(*Do not use "surely," which would actually cast doubt on the speaker's conviction.*)

Если не пойдем на уступки, мы оппозицию <u>просто-напросто</u> уничтожим.
If we don't go <u>wobbly</u>, we will crush the opposition, <u>you'll see</u>!

Since the dictionary equivalent of просто-напросто is just "*simply*"—not nearly strong enough—this colloquial intensifier has been tackled as follows: 1) by using a verb just as graphic as уничтожим, and 2) further compensating with an expressive colloquial word, "*wobbly*," while 3) the extra words (justified by the context) provide end weight, making up for the one-syllable unit in English, "*crush*."

Именно belongs in this category when used as in the following examples:

А <u>именно</u> здесь и надо искать ответ.
That is <u>exactly</u> where we must look. (*lexical solution*)
And <u>it is</u> here that we should be turning for answers. (*syntactical solution*)

Именно это я <u>и</u> сделал.
That's what I did do. (*grammatical solution*)

Or take the following sentences, where additional words are added for emphasis. When именно is an intensifier in the original, an English intensifier such as "*just*," or a syntactic ploy, such as beginning the sentence with "*it is*," might be appropriate.

Именно ему пришлось расплачиваться.
It was he who had to *pay* / *take the consequences*.
It was he who would be punished.

Since the verb in the original is clearly meant figuratively, as otherwise it would probably have been платить, the variants given above provide more detail.

Именно в тот момент зашел ее отец.
Just then her father walked in.
It was then that her father walked in.
But at that very moment her father walked in.
At that moment, who should walk in but her father!/?
And wouldn't you know it, that's when her father walked in.

When "именно" is used to mean "*namely*," it has largely become desemantisized, so can therefore safely be omitted, with or without compensation.

"Не забудь лекарства—(а именно) валерьянку и аспирин."
"And remember to take your meds—(I'm talking about) the valerian (drops) and the aspirin."

Emphasis, or the lack of it, for easier reading

The best overall plan is to use emphatic words or snappy idioms sparingly per paragraph. Try to limit them to places where they will not distract from words that the author himself deems important, judging from his Russian text. It is helpful to recognize words that have lost much of their semantic power in Russian, such as бороться , which used to mean "*struggle*," but now is usually closer to "*work for*," or even "*try to do*" something. Except when referring to an actual battleground in wartime, authors usually use some intensifier, as in настоящая/сущая борьба, баталия, when referring figuratively to a non-military struggle. This could be rendered as a *regular* or *pitched battle* or *battle royal*. Or take крупнейший, once always translated as "*the largest*," now often only "*major*," or even just "*large*."

Repetition

Repetition is yet another technique frequently used for emphasis. Whether or not to repeat a word is a problem the translator faces fairly often. As long as the same word is not used twice in the same sentence, which is taken to be bad form in Russian, words that are in constant use tend to slip by a Russian reader. However, if the English equivalent is not in frequent use in original English writing, it is sometimes better to use a pro-form (substitute): a synonym, pronoun, title, or attribute. This procedure must be used in news write-ups featuring a political leader, since it is considered disrespectful to use the pronoun alone. Yet that ban can be carried too far, and some papers today are opting for "*he/she*."

     Key words and supporting (auxiliary) words can be repeated for parallel structure, for emphasis, or to avoid unsuitable substitutes or ambiguity. But this does not necessitate carrying over every repetition found in the Russian original.

Repetition can be used in a wide variety of ways. The translator can repeat:

1. in related sentences (e.g., question – answer)
2. for rhetorical effect
3. if a synonym would be confusing/misleading/ambiguous
4. if a synonym that is not a keyword would call too much attention to itself; rather than using "elegant variation" for a neutral element, repeat it to avoid distracting attention from the key word

On the other hand, when repetition of the same word is not desirable, a proform—a substitute word or expression that stands in for or expresses the same content as another word or phrase—is a useful option. Independent of the form in the Russian, this could be:

1. a personal or demonstrative pronoun (*he, it, this*):

> Ваше поведение вызывает гнев и возмущение. Подобное поведение не прощается никогда.
> Your behavior makes us all very angry. It is absolutely unforgivable.

2. a relative pronoun or adverb (*which, who, whose, where*):

> Мария, моя сестра-историк, часто со мной общается по телефону. Машу интересует история нашего деда.
> Maria, my historian cousin who is always looking for facts about our grandfather, often talks to me over the phone.

3. someone's title, with or without a surname:

> Королева Елизавета выступила с речью. Она была, как обычно, немногословна, а ее слова были приняты с энтузиазмом.
> Queen Elizabeth gave a speech, brief and well-received, as Her Majesty's usually are.

4. omitted altogether by recasting the sentence; in this example, instead of repetition providing emphasis, a key word occupies a key (final) position in the sentence:

> Жена президента сегодня принимает множество гостей. Она всех, каждого гостя, радушно встречает.
> The First Lady will have a great many guests (in) today, with a warm greeting for each.

5. a more generalized word that refers to a word or phrase appearing earlier in the sentence or text (here the word is "*something*"):

> От него такие нападки всегда можно/надо ожидать. Нападки – это просто его стиль
> You can always expect such vilification/abuse (from him). That is something that comes naturally (to him).

There are two other possibilities—these depend on a broader context:

6. A word from the context that approximates the meaning of a previously occurring word

7. A synonym or a word from one's own terminological store/memory on a similar subject

How to tone down a sentence – and why

Toning down a sentence is sometimes necessary in translation for several reasons, including these two:

1. Words that, if not altered, would seem like overemphasis in English, and are too aggressive for what the author intended, judging from the context.

2. Overuse in Russian, resulting in stronger and stronger substitutions or modifications by an author apparently unaware of the effect his text may have on a foreign reader.

If a Russian modifier is in the superlative, but has become desemanticized from frequent use and no longer has its dictionary force for the Russian reader (it is referred to as an elative), don't hesitate to tone it down for the English reader, or even leave it out if the meaning—and character—remain essentially unchanged.

целый ряд ... is such an example of desemanticization in Russian caused by over-use, and should nearly always be toned down in English using *"several," "a number of," "numerous," "many," "a quantity,"* or *"some"* or just the plural of the noun.

But superlative or "elative"—which is it now? The Russian elative has the same form as the superlative, but implies no comparison, merely expressing a stepped-up version of the positive degree of the modifier. Старейший, крупнейший, богатейший, тяжелейший, or самый plus an adjective—all such modifiers in the superlative form require interpretation in English based on the actual degree of emphasis intended by the author, as you perceive it, in the original text. Is it really superlative? Look for the answer, first of all, in the immediate context. If it says "из всех" that suggests comparison: "ты у меня лучшая из всех / самая лучшая," or if it gives a helpful date, location, or other details, you are safe using the superlative in English. "Крупнейший завод," however, is ambiguous. If the context does not supply the required information such an adjective would be called an elative. Wherever possible, reduce the strength of the adjective one or two degrees, for example, for "старейший" use *"very old," "older"*, or just *"one of ..."*, as in *"one of the oldest museums,"* or use a substitute expressing "muchness" that does not entail degree, e.g., *"a major industrial center," "a great collection," "a treasure house/trove,"* or say, to satisfy convention, *"the veteran actress."*

These superlative-elatives, which "intensify" only on the surface, can be dealt with by either reducing the degree of the modifier in English or by using some other expressive word, for example:

человек широчайшей эрудиции
a (truly) erudite person; a man/woman of deep/extensive learning

принимает самое активное участие
is (very) active in…; actively campaigns (for) (*as per context*)

из самых разных уголков страны
from across the country; from all over (the country)

Using modals and "modals"

If one were to redefine "modal" for the translator, the broadest sense possible would include, but not be confined to, the grammatical (*may, might, can, could, would, should*). A personal element here serves to mitigate, soften, or make more tentative the dictionary equivalent of a Russian word. Such fine tuning can bring the standard English (dictionary) equivalent closer to the Russian original, or to what we perceive to be the author's intention. In different contexts our definition might extend to such closely related synonyms as minimizing, moderating, and making milder or less intense. As minimizers, mitigators, and softeners, "modals" make for a calmer, more tactful, diffident, or tentative presentation.

The opposite of intensifiers, such expressions tend to soften a statement, make it less aggressive or assertive, less blunt or "bald." Though they serve many purposes, the primary one is to play down a formulation in the original that does not reflect the author's intent, often because his words have been so overused that they no longer have the same effect on a Russian reader as they once did, so that stronger and stronger words tend to come into play. Cultural considerations play a part, too, as what looks shocking or overwrought in translation may well not seem so to a Russian. At the opposite end of the scale, what might look excessively polite, almost groveling to English speakers, is routine courtesy to a Russian.

For ведь, ordinarily an intensifier, there is a "modal" function as well. Instead of "*proves*," or "*is*," or "*as we know*," try a more tentative "*looks like*," "*shows signs of*," or "*has all the earmarks of*," any of which appears to tone down the original, but by calling attention to the sentence in this way, actually emphasizes the point:

Ведь это же фальшивка!
Well, if that doesn't look like a forgery!

Ведь ни для кого не секрет, что …
We do know, don't we, that …?
It's a pretty well known (fact) that … (*instead of the decades-old "the whole world knows"*)

Это <u>наверняка</u> самый худший наш сезон.
This is <u>probably</u> the worst season we have ever had.
(cf. another device, the <u>rhetorical question</u>: *"When did we ever have a worse season?"* or *"Has there ever been a worse season?"*)

Он <u>явно</u> думает, что мы ничего не понимаем.
He <u>seems</u> to think we don't know what he's up to.
(*"Seems" could be used instead of the more common "clearly" or "obviously," which may appear as too assertive. It does put across the force of the original, but without insisting.*)

Modals or "modal" expressions are polite: Such words and phrases can be used in English to express the deference implied in Russian politeness formulas.

Вы не подскажете, как пройти к музею ...?
Could you tell me how to get to the museum?
Excuse me, how do I get to the museum?
Which way is the museum, would you show me?

Вы не помогли бы мне, кто здесь лучший врач?
Excuse me, could you help me? Who is the best doctor around here?
(*a whispered request in a waiting room*)

Не прослушаете эту певицу?
Would you see your way (clear) to giving her an audition?

Вы не взгляните? Я набросал в тезисном порядке.
Do you mind glancing through some ideas I've outlined here?

<u>Не</u> найдете ли время взглянуть?
<u>Не</u> нашли <u>бы</u> вы время?
Could you (find time to) take a look at this?
Do you think you might (find time to) take a look at this?

This may sound obsequious, but to a well brought up (культурный) Russian, it may be merely the most accepted formulas for addressing a superior (or someone he needs to impress). Note the de rigueur negatives.

Now picture a crowd going in to a hit show or pop concert, where there is always someone frantically seeking that elusive "extra ticket." This is one place the "modals" would definitely <u>not</u> come into play. The super-politeness of the first version below would never ever be heard. The variants in the second version (good illustrations of emphatic devices besides) are much more likely.

В случае, если у кого(-либо) нашелся бы лишний билетик, я тут же с радостью (его) купил бы.
If anyone by chance discovered a ticket he or she did not need, I would happily buy it from him or her.

Есть лишний билетик? / Лишний билетик есть? / Билетик лишний есть?
Anyone got an extra ticket?
Got a ticket?
Hey ... excuse me! Ticket?

"AGENDA" —

ATTITUDE, POINT OF VIEW, VALUE JUDGMENT, IMPLIED MESSAGE

What the author had in mind—every step of the way—should be evident from his choice of words. Our job as translators is to decipher what lies behind those words. Has he written his text in a clear and transparent way? Or is there an implication lurking somewhere? Actually, his words will give you the clues you need to answer such questions. But an effort should definitely be made to discover which of his words provide the necessary information.

Favorable – objective – unfavorable

Is there evidence of the author's opinion/bias? Or does he seem to be objective? To put across in your translation the general tone of the sentence/text, and the connotation of a component, try to detect differences of tone in the Russian, as in the following examples:

Решительный отказ. (*strong and expressive, but except for the last variant, it could be used in a context that is generally objective*)
All they got from us was a firm rejection.
We emphatically/categorically rejected that.
Their offer was turned down in no uncertain terms.
We just said no.
"N-o, NO."

безапелляционное заявление (*strong and definitely unfavorable*)
... peremptorily announced
... stated in a most imperious way

категорическое несогласие. (*strong, but still comes across as objective*)
I absolutely disagree.
I must express my total opposition.
I beg to differ. (*short and sweet, probably "categorical" enough without translating the intensifier*)

But there are times when no nuance seems possible; it's either all good or all bad:

Это замечательный человек.
He is a wonderful person.

Какая чудная/чудесная погода!
What marvelous weather!

Что за чудный голосишко слышу я откуда-то!
I hear a sweet little voice in the distance!

Не буду пресмыкаться перед ним, не буду и все!
I absolutely refuse to grovel!

Sometimes a nuance expressing doubt, fantasy, etc. is introduced with a particle: будто, якобы, де, мол, дескать.

Он утверждает, будто вы к нашей победе не имели никакого отношения.
He claims you had nothing to do with our victory.

Мне снилось, будто/что мы идем по узенькой лесной тропинке.
I dreamed (that) we were walking down a little path through the woods.

Дальнейшее развитие (дела), дескать, зависит полностью от нас.
  (*implies doubt in another's judgment or sincerity*)
The rest, he claims, is entirely up to us.
According to him, what happens next depends on our decision.
The ball, he contends, is in our court now.

Она де устала и не придет.
She said (to tell you) she was tired and would not come.
(*The English in this translation could be objective, though the Russian is not, but in the variant below, the doubt is unmistakable.*)
She is too tired to come, (so) she says.

In a favorable-objective-unfavorable, step-by-step downgrade, from approving to scornful:

сговорчивый	reasonable, cooperative, moderate, helpful, willing to compromise
покладистый	obliging, easy(-going)
податливый	compliant, tractable
послушный	obedient, docile
покорный	meek

(излишне) мягкий   soft (*as in*: soft on crime, etc.), gentle, mild

мямля   wishy-washy, a wimp

Two Russian words related in appearance and meaning, but virtually opposite in tone, the "-анство" suffix is enough to completely change the point of view— and the sense:

Зачем нам такая критика – это же просто критиканство.
What kind of criticism is that?
That's just nit-picking. We would welcome an honest critique.

Здесь нужна политика, а не политиканство.
We need clear-cut policies, not politicking.
We can't (just) go on playing politics!

Favorable
Они работают рука об руку.
They march. / They work shoulder to shoulder.
Они работают не покладая рук.
They work tirelessly.

Unfavorable
Можете быть уверены, они давно спелись и всегда заодно.
They got together long ago and always work hand in glove, *you can be sure of that / so don't be surprised.*

Objective
Они хорошо спелись, работают слаженно, без разнобоя.
They work well together, always in sync.

Favorable
Она всем без (всякого) предубеждения подает руку.
She'll shake hands with everybody. (*no bias or prejudice*)

Unfavorable
Она кому угодно подаст руку.
Она кому надо подаст руку.
She will shake hands with *anybody / every Tom, Dick and Harry / anyone she needs.*

Objective
Потом она всем подавала руку.
After that she shook hands all around.

Irony and sarcasm

Irony must be recognized to be translated. When you detect some implied disbelief or irony, even sarcasm, in the tone of the original text, there are various ways of dealing with your discovery:

... муссируют возможность ...
they refer <u>gravely</u>—and <u>repeatedly</u>— to the possibility that ...
or
they keep harping on the possibility of/that ...
(*The ironical tone, implying "exaggeration," is here put across with two adverbs, the first unmistakably critical, the second referring to the multiple mentions that a subject usually gets in propaganda pieces.*)

те из вас, кто <u>свято</u> верит, что ...
or
вы, <u>правоверные</u>, полагая, что партия никогда не ошибается ...
you, the "true believers" who think that the Party can do no wrong
the "faithful" among you who actually believe that the Party can do no wrong
(*in case there is any doubt, the quotation marks clearly point to irony*)

Им необходимо создать <u>соответствующее</u> общественное мнение.
What they are aiming at is to create the (<u>necessary</u>) attitudes (they need).
They want to turn public opinion in the "right" direction.
(*Option 1 here already implies (borderline) negative, but compare with outright disapproval expressed through quotation marks in Option 2: in the "right" direction.*)

эта, с позволения сказать, идейка ...
this "idea," if you want to call it that ...

образчик
a nice example; one sweet example

статеечка
his lovely (little) article

газетенка
the (sensational/well-known) tabloid
(*"rag" would fit the bill, too, if it were not so dated, or if a dated term is appropriate in the context*)

Докатились до (такого) утверждения, (что) будто ...
They went so far as to allege ...
They actually claimed that ...

Вот до чего докатился!
Oh, that you should have sunk so low!
(*note exaggerated literary style in English*)

А мы-то! До чего мы (сами) докатились?
And what about us? Has it come to this?
(*cf.* пришли к такому выводу, *neutral, non-emotive, which would be
translated as:* "... came to the conclusion that / the conclusion was ...")

One and the same word can, of course, be seen from different angles. The intent
could well be straightforward, as in the next examples:

в очередной раз / очередной провал / очередная ошибка
the next time; the latest failure (in a series); yet another; yet again

Or else, look out for an ironical tinge:

Это – очередная история (о чем-то)
yet another case; (more of) the usual; same (old) thing (all over again)

Loaded words and implication

простые смертные/обыватели *vs.*
рядовые/простые (американцы, etc)
Unless the tone in the original is ironic or downright sarcastic, it would be better
not to say "*mere mortals*", and rely instead on "*the layman,*" if it is a popular
science text, or "*the man in the street,*" "*the average (American)*" or "*(just) ordinary citizens,*" "*the general public,*" as more neutral, yet informal enough for
other genres. Unless there is a good reason, avoid the narrowly U.S. colloquial
"*folks*" or other U.S. or British slang.

пресловутый / печально известный
If "*notorious*" is too strong (for what, according to the context, you perceive is
the author's intent), try "*the same old ...*" or other milder words of disapproba-
tion, including even "*that well-known...*"

хваленый
Use "*much touted*" (<u>not</u>: "*highly praised*" or "*praiseworthy*") as it will put across
the rather disapproving tone in the original; owing to its use in so many critical
articles, "*to tout*" today does not usually sound objective.

Я посмотрела, они (действительно) играли в карты.
I looked inside and saw they (actually) were playing cards.
(*objective, matter of fact*)

Я все таки посмотрела, <u>а</u> они (и вправду) <u>режутся</u> в карты!
I did look, and there they were, sitting around the card table (again)!
or
I did look and what do you know? There was the bunch of them at the card
table (like you said)!
(*emotional, because of the* <u>а</u>, *implying surprise or even disapproval; also*
режутся (*which does mean "playing," too*) *is not only colloquial, but
emotive/emphatic because of the tense jump in Russian. The main thing is
to spot the irony in the original so as to reflect it in the translation.*)

Make sure you understand the implication: is it neutral or loaded?

В России говорят … / Русские говорят …

The original is neutral in tone, so do <u>not</u> translate as: "*the Russians are saying
…*" which implies disbelief. If the original text has no such implication, use:
"*The Russians say.*"

В своем последнем выступлении …

This is neutral in tone, so do <u>not</u> use "*in his latest (public) pronouncement,*"
which might be suspect as to motives; better to say "*speech.*"

Они <u>внушают</u> нам, что выступают/ратуют за большие перемены.

Note the imperfective here, implying that "*they*" should not be believed.
Translate as: "*They would have us believe …*"
(cf. Они <u>внушили</u> нам/ <u>убедили</u> нас (в том), что … "*They convinced us that
they are for change …*")

Variations on the theme of "blah-blah-blah"
The following examples illustrate an author's attitude regarding the manner of
speaking:

<u>разглагольствовать</u> (о чем)	hold forth; talk long and loud (about/on…)
разглашать	trumpet
<u>болтать</u> (о чем)	babble away (about …); go on and on
"Хватит! Не болтай!"	"Stop (your nonsense)!"; "(Just) Shut up!"
заниматься болтологией	indulging in the worst kind of twaddle

Не слушай его, он (же) тебе просто <u>зубы заговаривает</u>.
Don't pay attention. He's trying to put one over on you.
Don't pay attention. He's trying to pull the wool over your eyes.

трещать	jabber, yatter, yakking (away)

"Только и слышишь—трещат целый день!"
"Chatter, chatter, chatter—*all day long / that's all you hear!*"

трепаться
"Что ты переживаешь/нервничаешь/психуешь? Она просто любит
   трепаться. Не слушай ты ее!"
"Don't get upset! She can go on and on—she'll say anything! Don't listen to
   her!"

n another context, what follows is more like friendly banter between two close
women) friends:

"Позвони мне вечерком! Потрепаться хочется."
"Give me a call tonight! We can gossip a little."
"Give me a call tonight! We can chat a bit/awhile."

Other words signaling disapproval, often ironical, are:

Возня (*rarely today*: мышиная возня; *popular with Soviet journalists*)
all the talk; uproar; brouhaha; row; fuss; hue and cry

шумиха (*more frequently*: шум) (*all with* по поводу)
ballyhoo; hullabaloo "over something" or "over nothing"

All the above can often be used with вокруг (чего-то). Compare with гнев,
негодование – "*outrage*," "*public outcry*," words that would be used in a serious,
non-ironic context.

Diminutives and augmentatives

Another way of changing the reader's perception of a word is with certain suffixes. Very common in Russian, such words are notably lacking in English, where
the few exceptions are, practically speaking, confined to the "-*y*" / "-*ie*" or the
dated "-*ette*," "-*let*" and "-*kin*" endings, and are applicable to only a small number
of basic units. Semantically, Russian diminutives and other altered words are
often highly loaded, but a different context can reverse the original implication:

друг / брат
дорогуля / дорогуша   sweetie, sweetheart, dear, honey, baby

дружок / дружочек / братец   bud, buddy, chum, pal, (my) friend
(*These can be used casually, in a friendly way, to man, woman, or child,*
   regardless of gender, but also, and mainly, ironically.)

друг and дружище
could be rendered as "man," *or even* "hey, you!" *as long as it fits in with the style of the context*

ноги

Ах, какие <u>ножки</u>!   (Wow!) What (beautiful) legs!
                                 Some legs!

Дай <u>ноженьку</u>, сейчас оденем туфелечек!
Give me your footsie/tootsie! We're going to put on your little shoe now.
(*an old grandmother simulating baby talk*)

Дайте-<u>ка</u> сюда <u>ножку</u>, сейчас ее помоем.
Let's have that foot now. We've got to get it washed (up).
(*nurse's aide to patient; note the formal verb ending, a bow to convention, although the "-ка" attachment keeps the tone informal*)

голова

Поверните/Поверни-ка сюда <u>головку</u>.
(Could you) turn your head a bit for me?

А! / Вот так! / Во! Теперь будем снимать.
Good / That's it — now we can shoot.
(*photographer to model; note the two modal verbs in English, also the transferred epithet*)

While it is mostly diminutive nouns that are featured above, adjectives and adverbs can also appear in diminutive form:

Да, и спасибо за <u>тепленькое</u> одеяло/одеяльце!
Oh, yes, and thanks for the blanket. Very nice and warm!

О это точно <u>мамочкин</u> сыночек!
Ooh, he's mamma's little boy, aren't you, baby?
Or in a very different situation:
Oh, he's <u>a mamma's boy</u>, all right!
(*The connotation—doting or ironical—will depend on the context: who is speaking, about whom, and how old is the "boy."*)

А <u>вечерком</u>, давай пойдем погуляем, а?
And tonight let's go for a walk, *shall we / okay*?

Подождите <u>малость/немножко/немножечко</u>, сейчас будет готово.
Wait just a bit. It'll be ready in a minute.

Давайте, одевайтесь, <u>быстренько</u>!
Come on! Get dressed, quick-quick-quick!

Common augmentative suffixes also produce an emotional effect that can be carried over into the translation:

ветер
"Ну, и ветрище!"   "What a wind!"; "What a weather!" (*colloquial*)
(*This as contrasted with the diminutive form*: ветерок *or* ветерочек "*a pleasant breeze.*")

голос
"Вот так голосина!"   "Wow! Some voice!"
                             "(Hey!) That's (real) lung power!"

Compare with the diminutive form:

голосок / голосочек / голосишко   a soft/sweet voice
(*In a different context, on the opera or concert stage, for example, where a microphone does not come with the job, this "sweet" sound could be described pejoratively, as "small," definitely "inadequate" for the venue.*)

дом
домище   a huge house; a New Russian's McMansion

Вот в этом домике я росла.   This is the house I grew up in.
(*A diminutive here would have either an emotional/nostalgic tinge or merely refer to the small size – the context will determine that.*)

Он построил себе домик в лесу.   He built (himself) a cabin in the woods.

Yet another suffix can have a minimizing effect. Words ending in –оватый hark back to the root word, but reduce its strength, and can be rendered in English in a variety of ways:

Он парень туповатый (from тупой).
He's *sort of dim / rather slow / not too clever*.

Кожа желтоватая (from желтый)
The skin *is yellowish / has a yellow cast*.

Ухажер у нее франтоватый (from франт).
Her boyfriend is a bit of a dandy.

Не знаю, не знаю … вид у него какой-то жуликоватый (*from* жулик).
I just don't know … do you think he's on the up-and-up?

He looks shifty-eyed to me.
He's a sort of shady character.
(Жулик *and its derivatives, however, are often used affectionately,*
  especially when addressing children, cf. "rascal" in English.)

Not all words with this suffix are in the same category. For example, with аля-
поватый ("*tasteless*" or "*cheap-looking*"), describing a crudely made object, we
seem to have lost sight of the root it was derived from (unless it be "ляп," as in
делать что-то тяп-ляп—to do something "*any old way*," or perhaps оказалось,
у него было много ляпов—"*turns out there was blooper after blooper*").

Diminutive forms of names
Personal (given) names, with all their variations, present a special kind of challenge. In addition to the first and/or last name that an American reader might expect, or a Russian patronymic (middle name), or a nickname, there is the wide
(and some would say "wild") variety of diminutives in use in various situations,
e.g., for Мария: Маша, Машка, Машенька, Машкин, Машутка, Мариванна
(humorous phonetic spelling for Мария Ивановна), then there is: Маруся, Ма-
руська, Муся, Мусенька (that's nearly a dozen already.) Other names have even
more variants, with intimates, friends, and relatives, as well as mean-spirited
journalists happily contributing to the mix. Short of disregarding these when
translating dialogue or letters, for example, which is where they tend to occur,
you either resort to footnotes, or compile a general introduction listing all the
variants contained in the original. Then again, you might, like many translators,
give up trying and just transliterate, or keep repeating the same "generic" ID
name so as not to further confound the reader.
    Other diminutive forms deserve the translator's careful attention, as the sense,
and more particularly the "sub-sense," varies with each particular context. The
"-ка" and "-ик" suffixes, for instance, although they primarily indicate familiarity
with the person spoken to or object referred to, have many variations in that relationship or viewpoint, ranging from scornful or deprecating:

идейка (*from* идея) – a paltry/insignificant idea
бумажка (бумага) – (*about a document deemed unimportant, through neutral*)
курилка (курительная комната) – smoking room
книжка (книга) – book
столик (стол) – little table

all the way to warm and affectionate:

детка (дитя) – baby, babe (*to an adult*)
деточка (дитя/ребенок) – sweetie (*to a child*)
детки/детишки (дети*) – referring to*: the kids
зайчик (заяц) – bunny (*whether applied to a young rabbit or as a tender
    form of address to a child*)

мальчик – boy (малец *today enjoys only limited use, even though it too is in a diminutive form*)

An option that may be available, similar to the ones recommended when rendering the formal "вы/Вы" and informal "ты," is the use of the device known as compensation. But the translator who rushes in ahead of the angels needs to know what he is doing, how his solution may influence the reader's impression of the text (or of a character, say, in a human interest story) where the "ты – вы" difference might be important. The idea is to offset a translator's understandable failure to find a dictionary equivalent for what would seem a simple enough problem.

Diminutives, however you look at it, are difficult to render into English, but the translator has to make an effort to cope with them. One plea: don't give up, and whatever you do, don't use "*little mother*" for матушка!

Despite all their good work, the earliest translators of the Russian classics into English never adequately coped with diminutives. These cannot always be just "translated." They sometimes need compensation, or a different approach to the context. More often than not, a diminutive is not meant as a unit in and of itself. It can influence an entire text or a part of it by setting the stage for the attitude of the author or his characters. Nuances that vary from favorable (friendly, familiar) to unfavorable (hostile, mocking), in addition to the neutral (objective) function, referring merely to small size, amount, or degree, all can be reflected in a diminutive suffix, hardly noticeable on the page, but by implication, important in putting across the attitude of the author.

Вы or ты?

Back to being polite, and the challenge of translating the formal "вы" and the familiar "ты." Ordinarily, "*you*" suffices for both, and the translator can let the context take care of the reader's impression as to the difference in tone. However, if specific emphasis is being laid on that difference, as in the following examples, it would probably be wise to disregard the pronouns altogether and compensate by describing the situation:

"Давайте будем с вами на ты?"
"Isn't it time for first names?"
"Let's not be so formal."

But serving as another illustration of the need to compensate, there is a righteous fuss over a "ты" that would be hard to imagine outside of a textbook:

"Прошу вас, называйте меня на вы."
"I do not wish to be addressed in such a familiar way."
"Be so good as to call me *professor / doctor / by my name* (and patronymic)."
"Who gave you the right to be so disrespectful?"

If that prim-and-proper lady were really so put out, she would simply avoid speaking to the impudent fellow in the future, or give him a subtle hint through another student.

In a different scenario, there is the following example:

"С каких пор вы с ней на ты?"
(*a question from a concerned elderly relative*)

Note that there is ambiguity here on two fronts: "вы с ней" could be referring to "*him*," "*her*," or both, i.e., meaning: "*how long have you been so familiar with her?*" or else "*since when are you two so chummy?* or "*since when are you on such familiar terms?*", etc. As a matter of fact, the phrase "*since when*" (с каких пор), both in English and in Russian, either means "*how come?*" or refers to an actual time frame. The overall aim in such texts would be to follow through with either a more formal or a less formal style, as the context demands.

Grammatical modals
As for the more traditional function of a modal, namely its use as a verbal aux-iliary, this plays an important role for the translator, too. Other parts of speech and phrases can also be put to good "modal" use. When translating, the modal verb may frequently be needed:

1. Even if the Russian has no overt indication of modality:

   Я тебя отсюда <u>не вижу</u>.
   I <u>can't</u> see you from here.

   … что небезопасно
   … which <u>may</u> prove dangerous

2. If the Russian does contain a "modal" expression:

   Это, <u>возможно</u>, сильно повлияет на твои шансы получить то место.
   This <u>could</u> have a serious effect on the odds/chances of you getting that job.

   <u>Можно</u> предположить, эволюция (уже) достигла наивысшие свои формы.
   We <u>can</u> assume that evolution had (already) reached its highest forms.
   Evolution <u>may</u> have reached its highest forms.

   <u>Можно</u> ли что-либо <u>противопоставить</u> урегулированию (проблемы) ядерного вооружения?
   <u>Can</u> there be any <u>alternative</u> to an agreement on nuclear weapons?
   <u>Is there</u> any <u>alternative</u> to an agreement on nuclear weapons?

The English modal here works just as well as the modal expression in the Russian, but the stark choice envisioned in the (possibly) rhetorical question permits a non-modal solution as well. The same goes for the next example:

Что они <u>могут</u> противопоставить нашему предложению?
What do they <u>suggest instead</u>?

Его невзлюбили за то, что он <u>якобы</u> не сумел остановить распространение злых слухов.
He earned their disdain for <u>supposedly</u> failing to halt the spread of the vicious stories.

"Modals" are also needed to directly express or tone down an already restrained Russian expression to convey the author's intention:

Ну, как? / (Как) понравилось?	So how did you like it?; How was it?
Не ахти.	Not (very) much.; Nothing special.; So-so.
В общем, ничего.	Fair to middling.; Not (too) bad.
Вполне (прилично).	(Pretty) decent, I suppose.
В общем очень мило.	Well, all right, I guess.
А у вас такое бывает?	Does that ever happen with you? Do you ever get that …?
Не без этого.	Maybe, just a little.
Он, оказывается, пьет?	He's a pretty heavy drinker, is he?
Не без этого.	On occasion.; You might say so, yes.
А он, что ли, тогда был выпивши?	So he'd been drinking? Was he actually drunk then?
Что ж, очень может быть.	Could well be.
Знаете, чуть попозже	Not just now.; Not this minute.; In a bit, all right?

So what makes a word a "modal" or "minimizer"? It is mainly that the "true" (grammatical) modals—may, can, could, would, should—and a variety of "modal" expressions can be employed to play down language that is not in keeping with the author's intent—too strong, emotional, forceful, loaded. An important caveat: a translator should not necessarily reach for a "modal" whenever he sees a "strong," expressive word in the Russian. As with intensifiers, due account should be taken of a formal vs. an informal context.

Certain minimizing modifiers are sometimes used by over-cautious academic as "insurance," or more charitably, to facilitate the flow of ideas:

В статье (<u>достаточно</u>) отчетливо проведена его излюбленная тема добра и зла.
This could be translated more simply as:
His favorite theme of good and evil *is evident throughout* / *always shines through*.
or in a perfectly faithful rendition:
His favorite theme of good and evil does seem to shine through.

У его героя (<u>некоторый</u>) привкус самовлюбленности.
A tinge of narcissism does creep into his portrayal.
(*The word* привкус *is already translated "soupçon," "hint," or "tinge" so any translation of* некоторый *would signify "a tinge of a tinge," or "buttery butter," as a Russian would describe it.*)

Чувствуется <u>определенная</u> склонность к высокому «штилю».
He exhibits a tendency to the lofty peaks of oratorical style.
He tends to favor the lofty peaks of oratorical style.
(*In the sentence above the ironical tone gets across using loaded words without modifying* склонность.)

Подробно рассказано о его <u>педагогической деятельности, давшей искусству</u> книги <u>целую плеяду</u> первоклассных художников полиграфистов.
There is a detailed account of his <u>work as a teacher</u> who has <u>trained so many</u> first-class book designers.
(*This sentence has been toned down to avoid an impression of unnecessarily fulsome praise, though without sacrificing the enthusiasm.*)

Some "minimizing" device can be used in English to deal with what might seem to us like overblown rhetoric, though the Russian reader tends to gloss over it. And there are other reasons, too, for toning down a phrase or sentence. An insensitive translation can distort the foreign reader's reaction to a rendering of the original text:

благородный труд / человек / поступок
should not necessarily be "noble," but instead:
worthwhile work; worthwhile effort; high-principled person; magnanimous act; generous act; selfless act

At the other extreme, to avoid having the next example sound like a rant in English (though in Russian it may not come across that strongly), the translation is toned down, preserving some impression of objectivity by focusing on only two of the four units (underlined in the Russian) used to convey a negative attitude. The translator took this risk to prevent the text sounding too emphatic, but he could also have compensated by using a more expressive or explicit word further on in the text.

> Эта <u>газетенка</u> опубликовала <u>домыслы</u> <u>некоего</u> <u>так называемого</u> "<u>специалиста</u>", который <u>заявил</u>, что …
> This paper published the <u>allegations</u> of one "expert" *to the effect that I* *who <u>claims</u> that* …

Other rhetorical ploys for playing down or de-emphasizing include:

- shortening a second reference to a loaded word/phrase the next time it is mentioned
- condensing the sentence
- substituting a neutral pro-form
- changing the focus of the sentence
- changing the article
- relocating to make room for a key word

"Modals" for emphasis

One seemingly paradoxical choice a translator can make when a standard or dictionary equivalent sounds inadequate in English is the use of a modal verb, or a "modal" word/expression. This, of course, is a trick of rhetoric. For logically, to say that something *is* so would be more convincing than to say it *seems* so. Yet sometimes introducing an emotional or "personal" note, which after all, is a function of the "modal" expression, may call attention to the thought more effectively than would a direct assertion. Care must be exercised in the use of this rhetorical device, always in keeping with the intention of the author.

As a variety of the famous English understatement, a "modal" can be a subtle form of emphasis. Compared with more explicit forms, it is sometimes more effective than a direct statement. Russian, too, has a use for this device, inserting a "modal" expression that is not meant to be taken literally, with compensation in the form of extra emphasis, for example:

> Я, <u>кажется,</u> <u>ясно</u> сказал, что ни на какую такую экскурсию/прогулку я не поеду, называй ее как хочешь.
> I <u>thought</u> I made it <u>fairly</u> clear that I am not going on any such junket, joyride, or whatever you want to call it.

The sarcasm in the Russian has been laid on with a trowel, making the author's intention abundantly clear, thus giving the translator the freedom to follow suit. Yet more often than not, the translator has to deal with explicitly stated emphasis in the Russian, so that a modal expression will reflect the author's intention, but in its own subtle way, "modally."

RHETORICAL AND PRAGMATIC FACTORS

Just as accuracy and readability are inextricably linked in a good translation, two other factors, the rhetorical and the pragmatic, are closely intertwined as well. Both are employed to direct attention and, hopefully, evoke a response. Because there is so much overlap between the rhetorical and the pragmatic, no effort is made here to keep them separate, as both are necessary to protect the accuracy of the translation.

The difference between these two components of the translator's art lies not so much with what methods the translator employs, since all of them sometimes involve changes in content as well as in form. When the Russian original is stylistically faulty, the Russian reader can usually sort out apparent contradictions and non-sequiturs. But in the English, it is up to the translator to do this. Pragmatic changes can supply needed information or help to adapt the text in other ways so that the reader will be better prepared to take in the author's ideas. Rhetoric is useful to bring home his message through skillful manipulation of the form.

> Под этим документом приложили/поставили свою подпись/подписались 500.000 человек.
> *or*
> 500.000 граждан приложили/поставили свою подпись/подписались под этим документом.
> Half a million people signed the petition.
> The petition had half a million signatures.

Both English versions make an immediate impression because the number is spelled out (admittedly easy to do with a round number like this one) while placement of key words also plays a role. The concrete type of document comes from the context.

> Это был первенец отечественной металлургии.
> That was the first steel mill in the country.

The figurative (and therefore expressive/emotive) overtone in первенец (*"first born"*) is compensated for syntactically by taking advantage of the important final position.

Как <u>загремел</u> первый взрыв, так все вдруг и <u>переглохли.</u>
After <u>just</u> the first explosion/blast everyone suddenly <u>went deaf.</u>

The emotional, informal tone of the verb and indeed the entire utterance, is expressed through an intensifier ("*just*"), plus the idiomatic "*went*" + adjective. Otherwise, in a more formal context such as: "После первого взрыва, все вдруг оглохли," the translation could conform to a more neutral standard if need be: "The first explosion deafened everyone."

CHAPTER 4

HOW PROFESSIONALS MANEUVER
AROUND DIFFICULTIES

When your translation work is flowing along nicely except for the need to ɔok up a technical term or find a synonym to avoid repetition, there may be little eed for any advanced translation theory. Yet in some cases certain analytical ıethods can help. For example, when you are reading through your own trans- ıtion and don't like what you see. Either the going is jerky, all stops and starts, ·r it seems stiff and unconvincing, or else so bland it bores you to tears, and you ave little or no idea how to improve it. Take another situation: you can see noth- ıg wrong, but the editor is continually finding fault. This may be the time to dip ıto the translation theory evolved by professionals who have been through the ıill themselves. The professional translator's devices for maneuvering around ifficulties are methods worked out by generations of translator-theoreticians for ıse when needed:

1. antonymic (*using an antonym + negation, if needed*)

2. conversive (*switching the "actors" around and adjusting syntax*)

3. generalization (*substituting an unspecific or more inclusive term*)

4. specific (*substituting a concrete term*)

5. contextual (*making use of a word plucked from the sentence itself, from elsewhere in the text or from your own knowledge of the situation*)

6. compensation (*shifting epithets or making up elsewhere for the lack of an exact dictionary equivalent or the unsuitability, for whatever reason, of the "exact" equivalent*)

7. logical development / unfolding action (*seeing a move ahead, as expected in, or justified by, the situation. Use caution, however, because careless use of this device can lead to the translator's substituting his own ideas for those of the author, or simply to a concocted text, barely resembling the thoughts in the original.*)

1. Antonymic

Antonymic translations can prove very useful, each one approaching a situatic from the opposite angle from the original, though the meaning of the origin remains intact:

>*Instead of:* не делать
>*consider:* <u>refrain</u> from doing *or* <u>stop</u> doing (*without a separate negative wor* *such as "not," though "don't do" is sometimes the best choice.*)

>*Or, as in the classic interdiction:*
>По газонам не ходить!   Keep off the grass!

This tactic can be used the other way around as well, with the opposite of the ke word coupled with a negative, as in:

>однофамилец …   <u>no</u> relation (to) …; <u>not</u> related (to) …

Common antonymic translations include:

>с учетом / учитывать
><u>not</u> forgetting …

><u>Самовольное</u> застекление балконов <u>воспрещается</u>.
><u>No</u> glassing in of balconies <u>without a permit</u>.
>No installing glass <u>without a permit.</u>
>Unauthorized glassing of balconies is <u>not</u> permitted.

>… представляет собой исключительно <u>ненадежный</u> материал
>… <u>is</u> dangerously <u>tricky</u>

>… <u>отвергает</u> диктат сверху/извне, из другой страны / от кого-либо
>… <u>won't</u> take orders from above/outside/another country/anybody

>Он <u>не</u> предлагает <u>ничего</u> <u>нового.</u>
>He just offers more of the same.

>Не проходите мимо! (*on a poster*)
><u>Stop</u> and look! (This could be you!)

>Учтите, что мы <u>не одни!</u>
>You may not know it, but we <u>have company</u>!

>Я <u>всегда хотел</u> быть с ним рядом.
>I <u>never wanted</u> to leave his side.

><u>Не допускать</u> ввоз иностранных товаров.
><u>Keep</u> foreign goods <u>out</u>.

<u>стихийное</u> использование природы
<u>unregulated</u> exploitation of natural resources

... куда <u>менее трудоемки</u>
... are really <u>labor-saving</u>

Аппаратура <u>не уступает</u> мировому стандарту.
The equipment <u>is up to</u> world standards.
The equipment <u>rates as high</u> as any in the world.

2. Conversive

The conversive solution is one where the "actors" are switched around, and a Russian reflexive sometimes becomes an active verb in English. Other times the device can work as follows:

«Я (лично) вручил ей письмо.»
"I hand-delivered the letter." (*direct approach*)
"She got/took the letter from me personally." (*conversive*)

С начала года организация предоставила помощь и поддержку тысячам семей.
Since early January, thousands of families got the help they needed from the organization.

Отмечалось, что акценты смещены, не так проставлены акценты.
There was definitely a shift in emphasis.

В операцию были вовлечены все наличные силы и средства.
The operation involved all (our) available troops and weapons.

Книга будет представлена большой аудитории.
Readers will soon see this book.

Практика дала хорошие результаты.
Good results have been achieved with this new routine.

Походы в музей предоставят детям возможность приобщаться к высоким духовным ценностям (со всего света).
Thanks to these trips, our children can benefit from exposure to the finest, most uplifting art the world has to offer.

... чтобы цветение не прекращалось круглый год
... so that the garden was always bright

Перед народом поставлена новая задача.
The nation now faces a new challenge.

The following example combines the conversive plus antonymic:

> Далеко не все тогда понимали его поведение.
> His behavior was puzzling to many.

3. Generalization

Sometimes where a Russian verb is specific, the English translation is generalized to a less specific one or even a common "multi-purpose" Anglo-Saxon verb. The reverse is a common tactic in translations from English into Russian.

> Кто желает еще поучаствовать/участвовать и дальше, просим
> оставаться на месте.
> Those wishing to stay on, please remain in your seats.

Sometimes a more specific word will solve your problem of word choice, depending on the context.

4. Specific

> специалисты уверяют, что …
> the experts/doctors etc., (*as per context*) *assure us / claim that* …

> сотрудник Белого дома
> a White House spokesman
> spokesman for the White House
> a White House official/aide/staffer/staff member

> сотрудничать / сотрудник
> work with; cooperate; collaborate; contribute (to); be a contributor; be on the
> staff; *or specifically*: author, editor (*according to the context*)

> документ
> message, declaration, petition, passport (*as per context*)

> Б. назвал его искусство/деятельность подвигом.
> B. called his poetry/effort an act of courage.
> (*this translation also includes a contextual solution*)

> К нему пришли родственники.
> His mother and father are here (to see him).

> Спасибо, мы уже поели.
> We've had lunch, thanks.

The following example combines generalization and concretization in one sentence:

Исход наступления зависел от мужества воинов, искусства/мастерства командиров.
The **success** of the **operation** hinged on the courage of the troops and the **leadership (skills)** of the officers/commander.
(*"Success" is more specific than* исход; *"leadership (skills)" more specific than* искусства; *and "operation" more general than* наступления.)

5. Contextual

Since your translation is of a text, not just a sentence, it is necessary to keep in mind the whole – both content and style. It is legitimate to find and refer to information in the context, and your own experience, even if that particular item does not appear in the sentence you are currently translating.

Суть дела не в том, как и почему, суть в том, когда начнется работа.
The hows and whys are not so important. **What** *counts* / *is important* is when do we **launch the project**?
(*Note also the use of the related word "project" that would obviously have to be "launched" before the* работа *can begin.*)

Ему нельзя больше ничего брать на себя!
He has shouldered far too many burdens already!
He's been through so much already!

живой уголок
animal corner (*in a daycare center, for example*)

6. Compensation

Compensation may be the answer when a translator cannot find a good way to put across some component of the original. He can sometimes modify (as a shifted epithet) or add another element to aid comprehension in a different part of the sentence, thus making up for the original deficiency.

Одна из жизненно важных проблем—это удовлетворение возрастающих потребностей населения в продуктах питания.
One problem we need to tackle **urgently** is how to *satisfy* / *provide (for)* / *fill* the ever-growing need(s) of the population for food.
(*The essential meaning of the phrase needs compensation in the rest of the sentence.*)

Красной нитью через все повествование проходит мысль о том, что московская физическая школа сильна преемственностью, передачей эстафеты от одного поколения ученых другому.

Cutting across the entire book is the theme of continuity. Moscow's physics research community has been able to *pass the baton / hand its traditions down* from generation to generation.

7. Logical development + conversive

The result of an action indicated in the original text can be a good solution for the translator – and consequently, the reader – if this tactic is employed judiciously.

Там <u>организовали/наладили/освоили</u> производство нового аппарата.
They<u>'re putting out</u> a new device.
Production of the new device <u>is on line</u> (starting next month).
They <u>can now produce</u> the new device.

Статья <u>приподнимает завесу</u> лжи, которая долго закрывала правду от нас.
This article <u>exposes some</u> of the lies that we have been exposed to for so long.

In the example above, the result of "*lifting a curtain*" would be "*to expose*"; the prefix при- is rendered as "*some,*" as in: "*<u>exposing some (a few)</u> of the lies.*" That does not rule out the "curtain" version, which is satisfyingly graphic.

Ты мне подарил ручку.
I am writing this with *your pen / the pen you gave me*.

К деятельности комиссии <u>были привлечены</u> все лучшие силы (какие только имелись) в <u>стране, работало</u> около 200 крупнейших ученых и инженеров.
The commission was <u>made up</u> of some 200 of the <u>nation</u>'s <u>leading</u> scientists and engineers.

In the example above, toning down the long laudatory phrase does not diminish the impact when в <u>стране</u> is replaced by the more effective "*the <u>nation</u>'s*"; the common Anglo-Saxon (phrasal) verb is a result of <u>были привлечены,</u> so that <u>работало</u> is no longer necessary; the elative крупнейших is replaced by "*<u>leading</u>*" to avoid unintentional overemphasis in the translation

Transformation

В <u>тех краях сеют</u> пшеницу.
They are all/mostly wheat <u>farmers</u> out <u>there</u>.

In this example, <u>сеют</u> is transformed into "*farmers*"; В тех краях becomes "*<u>out there</u>.*" "*<u>All</u>,*" or the alternative "*<u>mostly</u>,*" is added for better flow, and keeps the translator from straying too far from the substance of the original Russian.

CHAPTER 5

ACHIEVING READABILITY

The Russians themselves have complained for decades about the shabby treatment their native language has been getting at the hands of writers of scientific, technical, and descriptive literature, e.g., instructions for product use, let alone official or legal documents, which are notoriously hard to read in any language. If the meaning in the original is blurred, a translator has a number of methods he can use.

RUSSIAN "ALL-PURPOSE" VERBS

One translation concern is the constant stylistic problem resulting from the overuse of abstract (vague, all-purpose) verbs such as осуществить "*to implement.*" An article in the highly regarded *Literaturnaya Gazeta* decries the officialese found in more and more Russian writing meant for ordinary readers, whose own language is beginning to suffer from frequent exposure to such pompous gobbledygook. The illustration given was that of an elderly man in a remote village saying to his equally elderly wife, "Послушай старуха, а не пора ли нам <u>осуществить засолку</u> огурцов?" which roughly comes across as "*Don't you think it is time to commence the cucumber-pickling process?*" The author calls attention to the noun-ridden, de-personalized, and generally stereotyped sentences that are stripping the richness and vigor from the Russian language.

The "*Literaturka*" author is particularly incensed by the substitution of that one seemingly all-purpose verb for a variety of specific verbs. The vague and overused verb осуществлять(-ся) requires an abstract or process noun to complete the sense. For hack writers, virtually anything can be "*implemented.*" His illustration, which he actually saw on a sign nailed to a fence, was: "Вход осуществляется через калитку," apparently designed for those entering on foot so as to avoid having to open the big gate for pedestrians. Any Russian catching sight of that sign would probably laugh out loud, unless he was already so inured to such language that he wouldn't even notice the aberration. The obvious solution would be to delete that ubiquitous verb altogether, leaving simply: "Вход через калитку."

Whatever happened to the useful and perfectly good specific verbs seen in a variety of contexts? The translator reading these lines might benefit from a Russian's exasperation over the way that uncaring, tone-deaf authors, perpetrators of mass verbal offenses, are despoiling the "great Russian language."

"Body Language" in Metaphor and Idiom

Not every translation requires a lighter tone. But where readability is prime, it is worth considering more informal, in fact, colloquial language. This is when the "body verb" comes into its own. Take care, however, not to change the meaning and not to let the body verb get out of hand in terms of correct grammar and usage. Don't overdo it.

Since this level of language exists in many cultures, it is not surprising to get texts for translation containing metaphors and idioms, some with "body parts' as actors. How satisfying to discover such a word in an original text and to succeed in matching it up with an English equivalent, though sometimes in a different form. This is quite difficult to do, though, when the original reveals no hint of a body verb. We start with those hard ones then, and suggest some solutions.

Профсоюзы сыграли существенную роль в проведении важного законодательства / важных законов.
The (trade) unions were instrumental in the adoption of important new legislation.
The (trade) unions were instrumental in pushing through important new laws.
The (trade) unions helped push through the new laws. (*the context has already told us they are important*)

Version 2 and 3 above show the step-by-step development of a way to simplify and "humanize."

Remember such useful items as the following, when you need them, as these verbs can be useful in a wide variety of contexts:

вмешиваться	poke one's nose into
приглядываться к / подумывать о	eye; play with (the possibility of)
выслушать	lend an ear; hear (me) out
не без участия ·	have a hand in
указывать на	point a finger at
выдать (кого-то)	finger (smb.)
подчиняться	toe the line
смолоть глупость	put one's foot in one's mouth
тянуть / задерживать	drag one's feet

Надо выдворять «нелегалов»!
We've got to kick the illegal immigrants out!

Посмотрим, кто первый дрогнет.
Let's see who'll be the first to blink.

Они на нарушения смотрят сквозь пальцы.
They just wink at such violations.
They look the other way.

Надо будет выяснить, (в чем дело).
I will look into it. (*as per context*)

Нельзя закрывать глаза на такое безобразие.
We cannot turn a blind eye to such an outrage.

На такой шаг его надо слегка подтолкнуть.
He needs a little nudge in the right direction.

От него вы тогда отвернулись.
You (all) turned your back on him.

А он ушел от нашего договора. / А пошел на попятную.
Well, he backed away from our deal/agreement.

В статье указывается/обращается внимание, как на преимущества, так
  и на изъяны программы.
The article points to both the advantages and the flaws of the new plan.

Тогда и начнут действовать таблетки.
or
Тогда и войдет в силу запасной вариант/план.
That's when these pills will kick in.
That's when Plan B will kick in.

Она обязательно встряхнет партийные ряды.
She is guaranteed to shake up the Party.

Нас эта новость потрясла.
We were badly shaken by the news.
or in a different context:
We were jumping up and down when we heard.
We were *blown away / absolutely amazed* when we heard.

Он всегда умеет отмахнуться от критики!
He can shrug off any criticism!

Ну, теперь что скажешь?
Chew on that, if you want!

Ведь такое подрывает уверенность в себе.
Things like that can eat away at your self-confidence.

Проинструктируйте меня, пожалуйста, шаг за шагом.
or
Вам надо будет это объяснить, шаг за шагом.
Walk me through that, if you would.

Придется вам проглотить обиду.
You'll have to swallow your resentment/pride.

На-ка, съешь! / Ну как, съел?
Take that if you can!
So, touché? (*a less violent variant*)

Ее легко склонить в любую сторону.
She is so easily swayed.

Нельзя пренебрегать такой важной проблемой!
or
Это! тебе не баран чихнул.
It's nothing to sneeze at!

Ты долго будешь смаковать свою участь/обиду?
You cannot wallow in self-pity forever! (*if justified by the context*)

А можно просто отделаться шуткой.
I just laugh it off. (*the "I" is in the context*)

Этот господин чуждается любых проблем.
This gentleman shies away from any problem at all.

ANGLO-SAXON AND PHRASAL VERBS

Sometimes there is an advantage to using ordinary, everyday words, including phrasal verbs, instead of the standard dictionary equivalent. If the context allows for some relief from one and the same style level, try inserting simpler words, such as the ever popular "*get*," as in the next three examples:

добиться принятия нового законодательства
instead of: being successful in promulgating legislation
help the potentially struggling reader by translating this as: getting the new laws adopted/passed.

он победил (на переговорах)
instead of: he was victorious at the negotiations
try a simpler way: he got what he wanted

привлечение женщин к участию в предвыборной кампании
(*This is yet another use of* -ение.)
instead of: enlisting *or* drawing them in
try a variant that might better "grab" the reader, such as: getting women involved in the election campaign

уважать	*instead of only:* respect
	sometimes use: look up to
отличать	*instead of:* differentiate
	try: tell (them) apart; tell "a" from "b"
различать	*instead of:* distinguish
	try: make out (smth/smb in the dark/distance)
сложить / складывать / монтировать	assemble → put together
сталкиваться	encounter → come across; run into
придерживаться	adhere → stick to
уменьшаться / снижаться	decrease → drop; slide; fall (off)

Необходимо форсировать ... процесс.
It is important to step up this process.

Наша страна заботится о свободе и равноправии всех народов.
Our country wants to see all nations free and equal.
Our country works for (the) freedom and equality of/in all nations.

(The context here would prompt the translator to decide between "wanting to" and "working for," since these are obviously not synonyms.)

Костюмы не соответствуют этому периоду.
The costumes do not *fit in with* / *belong to* this period/era.

учредить деловое сотрудничество
start up a business relationship; team up with; working together; collaborating

триумфальная арка, созданная в честь ...
an arch of triumph put up *to honor* / *in honor of* ...
(A common Anglo-Saxon verb often does the job better than the dictionary equivalent because "put up" in this sentence does not distract from the key words, as "created" might have done.)

занимать/придерживаться все более жесткой позиции
take an increasingly firm/tough/hard line
take a harsh stand
take an intransigent position
(The options vary from a generally approving stance to a clearly disapproving one.)

ACTIVE OR PASSIVE?

A translator sometimes pays little attention to whether the English verb he chooses is active or passive. So little, in fact, that even where the verb in the Russian original is active or reflexive (or where there is no verb at all) he may well put a passive in the translation. If this is justified, to direct the reader's attention to a key word, for instance, then well and good. But if the translator's passive form results from his failure to search for options, let him at least give the active voice a chance, make the necessary adjustments in the syntax, and judge which version comes across better

Consider the advantages of both active and passive constructions. Don't stick with the arrangement in the original if a variant is more effective in English. Take into account the meaning of the entire text rather than merely a single word, so that occasionally you can risk writing a sentence with the same sense (but different words and syntax), rather than being satisfied with just the one-word equivalents in the dictionary. One model to consider might be instead of saying "*is operated*" or "*is run*" say "*operates*" or "*runs.*"

Управление машины осуществляется на расстояние.
or
Станок <u>управляется</u> дистанционно.
The machine runs by remote control.

t's not that "*a machine operated by remote control*" is necessarily always wrong.
The aim is not to stop at the first word or form that comes into your head, but to
explore other options, too.

In the following sentence the absence of a verb points to an "*is*," or the translator
can recast the sentence:

Ход автомобиля ровный, бесшумный.
The car runs smoothly and quietly.
You get a smooth, quiet ride.

Дело <u>велось</u> из ряда вон плохо пока <u>не</u> пришел новый начальник.
The business was *not doing well* / *going under* until the <u>new manager
arrived</u>.

In the above sentence, note the (prescribed) use of the negative form in Russian
(пока <u>не</u> пришел …), which does not convey a negative meaning, nor does it
translate as a negative in English. The only negative in the translation is <u>not doing
well</u>.

Книги <u>расходились</u> быстро.
The books were selling well.

Оптимистический тон прогноза был обусловлен атмосферой доверия,
  / тем доверием, которое завоевал кандидат
The optimistic forecast grew out of the trust that the candidate had earned
  from (the) people.
The forecast was so optimistic because the candidate had gained/won (the)
  people's trust.

В музее <u>ведется</u> работа по изучению древних икон. Идут
  восстановительные работы.
The museum is making a study of old icons, with restorers already at work.

If a different sentence reads: В музее ведутся восстановительные работы,
without further information qualifying the action, then it would be the museum
itself that is being renovated.

За это (достижение) все трое были удостоены Нобелевской премии.
For this all three got/earned the Nobel Prize.

If the "achievement" has already been mentioned, "*this*" is all that is needed. The
passive "*were awarded*" should not be rejected out of hand. Try different versions
instead of always sticking to the form of the original.

The passive or "pseudo active" can sometimes be used to advantage, as in the following cases:

1. For prominent (final or unusual) placement of any sentence element, including agent:

    > Они уверены, что выиграли из-за того, что <u>сам</u> Бог им помогал.
    > They are certain that they won because they were *(being) helped* by / *getting* help from God <u>Himself</u>.

    Note the prominent final position for emphasis, end weight for balance, and the pseudo-active verb, which here is even more effective than the passive.

2. When a word from a previous sentence, or its replacement (a pro-form or synonym) is repeated at the start of the new sentence as a transitional element

3. To avoid repetition of the agent when the agent has already been mentioned here or within the immediate context

4. When the agent is irrelevant or intentionally ignored, and therefore not mentioned

5. When it is implied that the agent is someone in authority, then the verb is generally in the plural

    > Его <u>лишили</u>/сняли с поста.
    > He <u>was removed</u> from his post.
    > He <u>was stripped</u> of his post.

    > Их обвинили во взяточничестве.
    > They were accused of taking bribes.

6. When the passive nature, even helplessness, of a situation is being stressed (e.g., with the Russian impersonal active)

    > Но в этот раз его тяжело ранило.
    > This time he was badly wounded.

7. When the agent is implied in the context or his presence is clear from the situation

    > Его <u>освистали</u> (со сцены) /... <u>захлопали</u>
    > He was <u>booed</u> (off the stage).
    > He got the rapid hand clap treatment.
    > (*with or without a footnote or unobtrusive explanation of the different sounds that indicate extreme disapproval in different cultures*)

DELAYS AND INTERRUPTIONS

Careless writing sometimes pushes the key words into less than advantageous positions, causing at least momentary discomfort for the reader if this problem is carried over into the translation. Words and phrases can be relocated if advisable.

1. Long attributive phrases (in initial position)

> Действующие в прибрежных водах Филиппин пираты совершили нападение на пассажирский паром в районе острова Хиганте.
> Pirates operating in Philippines coastal waters have attacked a passenger ferry off Gigante Island.
> (*Always check place names and all other proper nouns not already familiar to you.*)

2. Long participial phrases (in initial position)

> Имея, как и всегда, самые благие намерения, он допустил оплошность прямо смехотворную.
> With/Despite all his good intentions, he put his foot in his mouth once again.

> в таком немаловажном для нас деле
> in a matter so important to us
> in such an important matter

3. Long "parenthetical" phrases or clauses

With delays, including a long attribute, move the attributive phrase to a position following the noun; a prop verb with process noun.

> Есть ли возможность достичь в течение переговоров в Женеве в следующем году основу для подписание такого договора?
> Is there a/any possibility / Is it at all possible that such an agreement can be reached at the Geneva conference / in Geneva next year?
> Could there be a basis for signing an agreement like that at the Geneva conference?

Below are two different meanings of средства in two translations, but both re-site the modifying phrase to follow the noun:

> ... всеми доступными ему тогда средствами
> ... by every means available (to him) then

> ... все имеющиеся у них в то время средства
> ... all the funds they had at the time

The attributive group below, instead of being relocated, has been merely shortened:

На сухой, <u>твердой как камень</u> земле, вырос цветущий сад.
On that barren, stone-hard earth they created a veritable garden in bloom.

Next, the long attributive phrase has been turned into a relative clause:

Он высказал <u>свое ставшее в последствии столь известное</u> утверждение.
That is when he made that claim/assertion, which has since become so widely known.

ADJECTIVE FORMS

To make the reader's job easier, try out different adjectival and other form modifier for a Russian phrase or single word in the genitive or other case:

• **Possessive**

А мэр Москвы уже прибыл.
Moscow's mayor had already arrived.

не вмешиваться в делах друг друга
not to meddle in each other's affairs

• **Hyphenated words**

новости на первой полосе / новости с первой полосы / главные новости д
front-page news

руководство «сделай сам»
a do-it-yourself manual

• **Prepositional phrase** (*of, at, in, on, from, before ...*)

Все средства мира не смогут возместить огромные потери.
All the resources in the world will not compensate for their terrible loss.

Стрелки часов указывали полночь. Нет, без десяти минут двенадцать.
The hands of the clock pointed to twelve. No, it was ten minutes to/of/before twelve.

первый день недели
the first day of the week

Национальный комитет США <u>по</u> тихоокеанскому экономическому сотрудничеству
National Committee on Asia-Pacific Economic Cooperation

Дебаты в США вокруг "мер доверия" в ядерной области
Discussion/Talks/Debate on nuclear confidence-building measures;
  Nuclear confidence-building talks

• **Modifying word following**

выходной день
day off

выходные
the weekend or holidays

• **Relative clause (*which*, *that*, or pronoun omitted)**

Тем, кто уже был на месте, выдавались билеты.
Those who had already arrived got tickets.
Those (who were) already there got tickets.

• **Noun as attribute**

ножка стула   chair leg

певчие птицы   songbirds

куриная ферма   poultry/chicken farm

документы с грифом «совершенно секретно»
top secret documents

• **Comparative degree of the adjective**

старые/престарелые жители
older/elderly residents/villagers/people; senior citizens; seniors

• **Adverb/adverbial phrase, with syntax adjusted**

Просим решить наш вопрос в ускоренном порядке
We request that our case be urgently/expeditiously reviewed.
We request that our case be treated as a priority.

• **Compound, hyphenated word as adjective**

Можно будет платить в рассрочку или же за каждую покупку на месте.
We *provide financing / have an installment plan*, so you can opt for a pay-
as-you-go arrangement. Or if more convenient, just pay at the purchase
site.

В Госдепе США введена должность посла <u>по</u> особым поручениям
The U.S. State Department has instituted the post of ambassador-at-large.

• **Solutions with variants**

английская королева / королева Великобритании
England's Queen; the Queen of England; the British Queen

интереснейшая книга
a book of consuming interest; a really exciting book; "I couldn't put it down."

люди самых разных профессий
people working in many different fields; a cross-section

• A redo where the form is imaginatively transformed, but the key word remains intact, for instance the phrase: соломоново решение. If translations like "*a wise decision*" or "*prudent judgment*" seem too weak (and you don't want to lose "*Solomon*" altogether, although this is clearly a reference to his wisdom, not to the biblical character himself) you could venture a solution of your own, something like:

"a decision Solomon himself might have reached"

• **Basic one-word adjective**

And finally, the "true" (basic) one-word adjective, all degrees, including the elative (superlative form, but with no comparison implied):

И машина как раз <u>красного цвета</u> стояла у подъезда.
And it was a/the <u>red</u> car that stood at the entrance.

Which article you use depends on the context: if it was an unknown, but expected red car, or a particular one that was both known and expected.

Or for instance "*crazy*":

Каждое новое решение казалось еще более безумным, чем предыдущее.
Each decision of theirs seemed even crazier than the last.

Some Russian Sentence Patterns

There are several typical patterns that should immediately raise warning signs for the translator:

1. Sentences beginning with a noun/pronoun in an oblique case (with or without a preposition). If it is a key word, it is sometimes enough to nominalize, with the appropriate adjustments in the syntax; if an auxiliary, there are more options. Experiment by testing out variations on the theme.

В парке <u>звучали</u> вальсы, польки.
In the park waltzes and polkas <u>were played/heard.</u>
(*awkward, with a disappointing "fizzling" ending*)
or
Waltzes and polkas <u>were played</u> in the park.
(*wrong stress on "park" instead of the key words—"waltzes and polkas"*)
or
<u>Strollers</u> in the park *<u>heard</u> (the <u>band</u> playing) / were treated to* waltzes
  and polkas.
(*Inserting some "actors," if the context permits, makes this last
solution an example of the conversive tactic.*)

Мне вскоре дали понять, что я (больше) не нужен.
It got to me fairly soon – I was not <u>wanted</u> (any more).
(*"Needed" would work in place of "wanted" here if the context were
neutral, but in this sentence, it is clearly emotional, hence this solution.*)

Никаких ценностей, кроме денег и наживы у них давно нет.
They have long since lost any sense of values except money and profit.

В интересах мира—отказ от всякого рода ядерного оружия.
Progress towards peace demands that all forms of nuclear weapons
  be scrapped.

2. A participial or long prepositional phrase at the start of a Russian
   sentence: how to understand and handle these and other formal
   constructions not frequently found in American English

   Будучи еще ребенком, он свободно владел китайским языком.
   Even as a child he was fluent in Chinese.

   Переделав главу уже в который раз, он наконец остался доволен.
   He edited and re-edited the chapter before he was finally satisfied.
   He revised the chapter again and again before he was finally satisfied.
   He went over it umpteen times before he was finally satisfied.

   Балуясь на роликах по мостовой, мальчишка не рассчитал
     скорость движения и попал под первую же машину.
   The boy was cavorting in the street on his roller skates and did not
     notice how quickly the oncoming traffic was approaching. He was hit
     by the first speeding car.

3. For passive, reflexive, and impersonal verb forms, experiment using the
   active voice with an agent from the context.

Надо отказаться от всякого рода удовольствий, забавы,
настаивают они.
You must renounce any kind of pleasure and fun, say the zealots.
(*as per context*)

4. An unfavorable noun-verb ratio: a preponderance of nouns, especially
"process" nouns, results in heavy going for the reader

Приведение в порядок этих документов – дело сложное, приведет
приводящее к переделке всей системы / к созданию
совершенно новой системы.
Getting those papers in order isn't going to be easy. It entails
reconfiguring the entire system.

There are several problems in this short sentence. The process nouns (При
ведение and переделке or созданию) need some reconfiguring of thei
own—here to verbals. The dash will be converted to "*is*," or rather, "*isn't.*"
The comma separating the two parts of the run-on sentence will become
period so as to avoid a run-on sentence in English. Finally, the repetition i
приведет and приведение, with slightly different meanings, sounds care
less even in the original. Remedy: start over and re-do the syntax of th
whole sentence.

5. With long qualifying phrases or adjective groups standing before the
noun they modify

Находящийся на левом берегу реки южнее Адлера дендрарий
привлекает туристов со всего света.
The arboretum (tree garden cum nursery) is located along the left
bank of the river south of Adler. It is a favorite spot for tourists from
all over the world.

6. Too many words, including attributive phrases, between the subject and
the verb, forcing the reader to wait—and possibly lose the thread—before
getting to the point.

Надо было заботиться о всяких необходимых, но и о совершенно
излишних, не входящих в его обязанность вещах.
He was supposed to *see to / deal with* all sorts of things, both
necessary and absolutely unnecessary, things that were totally
outside his line of duty.

Experimenting with syntax

In your search for the best solution, a flexible approach is useful:

- Change one part of speech at a time and adjust the rest of the sentence
- Change syntax entirely, adjusting parts of speech, and re-siting various items to achieve end weight if necessary
- Add items for end weight if desirable (non-meaningful or with little semantic information, from the context or from your general knowledge)
- Add meaningful items for an identifier or unobtrusive explanation
- Omit items if unnecessary for a U.S. reader or if obvious from the context
- "Audition" synonyms and make the necessary adjustments to the rest of the sentence
- Test different style levels to determine the most appropriate in the context

Once the meaning of the Russian is clear, set down whatever ways come into your head to express the same thought. Consider ignoring the Russian words and syntax altogether. Picture the thought and express it in English. Then start editing/paraphrasing your own translation.

Try different style levels/registers, choosing the most appropriate in the context. Sins of style are all too easy to commit. A misfit can creep up on you, though it can sometimes be put to good use. "*To strive,*" for example, sounds even more formal in English than "стремиться" does in Russian. If a more official-sounding text is required, then use "*strive.*" If a more informal style is required, then use "*try to*" or "*go for,*" etc.

For training purposes, regroup sentence elements, adjusting syntax and trying varied sentence starts. Consider whether a verbal construction in the translation should be active or passive, personal or impersonal. Each type has its merits to point up a key word or generally enliven a text, or to lead into or make room for the key words, which otherwise might get lost in the shuffle.

VERBOSITY – HOW TO AVOID IT

What leads to verbosity? Haste, usually. Or an unwillingness to edit one's work for conciseness, tightening up the translation, a process often necessary because Russian tends to be up to 30 percent longer than English. We should all remember that "easy writing makes hard reading." True, some constructions in Russian are long and many Russian words are polysyllabic. And Russian texts often have words that would be superfluous in English. This results in texts that can be so much longer than an original English equivalent would be. Why is it then that a Russian text hastily translated into English sometimes turns out even longer than the original? Probably because the translator:

- failed to take advantage of the more compact English constructions
- did not go over his work to weed out: repetition, redundancy, tautology
- was lax in spotting:
  - a) unnecessary identifiers, prepositions, transitions, etc.
  - b) combinations using process nouns and prop verbs
  - c) roundabout ways of saying things

What can a translator do to avoid an excessively long (and clumsy!) text in English? He can tighten up (compress) sentences and text:

- By omitting an unnecessary identifier or prop word

  (Винтовка) (типа) "Ремингтон" давно—много лет, как стала
  главным спутником охотника.
  The Remington (rifle) has been the hunter's principal companion for
  years.

- By using a shorter construction in English instead of the initial participial phrase in Russian; either compress the participial phrase itself or substitute a prepositional phrase or absolute construction, etc.

  (Выступая) в субботу на пресс-конференции, он призвал
  покончить с ...
  At Saturday's press conference, he called for an end to ...
  At Saturday's press conference, he called on ... to stop ...

  ... переговоры, (направленные на заключение договора по)
  прекращению огня
  ... cease-fire talks/negotiations
  (*This one also included the use of a hyphenated noun as an attribute.*)

- By reducing an introductory prepositional phrase to a single word

  (Во время того, как происходит) данный процесс ...
  During this process ...
  (*The whole* "во время ... происходит" *phrase here is only a prop and
  can be dispensed with or substituted for by a preposition or adverb.*)

- By using a "–*ly*" adverb.

  Таково самое лаконичное содержание нового предложения.
  instead of: This, in the briefest possible summary, is the substance of
  the new proposal.
  write: This, briefly, is (the substance of) the new proposal.

- By ridding the sentence of an unnecessary identifier or prop word(s):

  американский (<u>вариант</u>) английского (языка)
  American English

  главное препятствие (<u>на пути</u>) (<u>осуществления</u>) всеобщего и
  полного разоружения
  the main obstacle to general and complete disarmament

  переводя рабочую силу из сельского хозяйства в (<u>сферу</u>)
  производства и услуг
  transferring workforce from agriculture to manufacturing and services

- By combining sentences or clauses, tossing out empty verbiage:

  Инициатором ... выступил "X", предлагая ... .
  At the urging of "X"...; On X's initiative ...; X (has) urged ...;
  X was the first to propose ...

  Центральный музей (известен множеством замечательных
  картин). (Среди) экспонатов (музея) находятся (<u>полотна</u>) (<u>таких</u>
  <u>известных/ знаменитых</u> <u>художников</u>, как) Рембрандт и Ван Гог.
  Exhibits at the Central Museum include a Rembrandt and a Van Gogh.
  At the museum are paintings by Rembrandt and Van Gogh.
  The museum owns a Rembrandt and a Van Gogh.

- Where another construction might involve an introductory prepositional
  phrase + identifier, by transforming into a subject + verb:

  (Как сообщает агентство) Рейтер ...
  Reuters reports that ...

- Detecting and dealing with a tautology:

  Работа (построена) на (<u>основе</u>) единой концепции.
  The work is based/built on a single concept.
  (*choose either* построена *or* на основе, *as they cover the same ground*)

- If reader interest is desirable, omitting extra words again and concretizing
  the verb:

  археологи, <u>занимающиеся</u> (<u>проблемами</u>) палеолита
  archeologists *researching / exploring / studying / specializing in /
  concerned with* the Paleolithic

Be careful not to let enthusiasm for tightening up your translation get out of hand. Many texts do benefit from compression, but reducing a participial modifier all the way down to *"Paleolithic archeologists"* might be a bit misleading.

- By attending to "fillers" in the original:

Some authors, wishing to create a suitable pattern or a lively, interesting style, firmly attach a modifier or two to virtually every noun and every verb in sentence after sentence. That doesn't mean we have to do so. An intensi-fier, a synonym, or some other word conveying little additional information is often used by such an author just as extra syllables to balance out his sentence, as in:

яркий, красочный стенд
an impressive display; a (bright and) colorful display

Although яркий alone could mean *"outstanding"* or *"impressive,"* here the two words, to all practical purposes, are synonyms. The author's motivation, however, need not apply to the translation. We have our own concerns as to readability.

Whether such a manner of writing appeals to Russian readers is beside the point. Readers in the West are used to a tighter style, with the emphasis placed strategically, not scattered throughout the text. Barring texts where every word of the original must be reflected with a word in the translation (e.g., certain legal or technical texts), the task of the translator is to convey the meaning of the original, not necessarily its form. This requires a discreet approach, navigating between accuracy and readability, boldly removing obstacles to understanding, yet always remaining true to the substance and tone of the original.

- Finally, a conglomeration of problems in just one Russian sentence, definitely not to be carried over into the translation:

Богатое и разнообразное творческое наследие Циолковского, вобравшее в себя многие важные достижения прогрессивной социально-политической мысли России второй половины XIX – начала XX века, содержит ряд важных теоретических положений, имеющих большое значение для анализа не только перспектив развития мировой космонавтики, но и многих актуальных проблем и процессов современности.
(*1 sentence, 46 words!*)

Here we have a prime example of excessive verbiage – and it is not merely a matter of how many words in a sentence. Suppose you get an overblown text like this to translate. Be brave and dispense with the empty rhetoric. Get to the point, using more compact constructions and melding similar elements. Turgid prose has a tendency to turn the reader off. Always see to it, however, that no essential detail is lost. Consider this solution:

> Tsiolkovsky was clearly influenced by the progressive social and political philosophy of the mid 19th to the early 20th century. His theories are useful in analyzing important issues of our own time and he predicted the development of space flight.
> (*2 sentences, 39 words – and a sigh of relief!*)

Noun-verb ratio

A word count in your translation is a useful tool that may lead to some grammatical transformation and can help make a dry, impersonal, or obscure passage easier to read. The idea is to find the proportion of nouns and verbs in a sentence or paragraph, and if there is a preponderance of the former, especially "process" (verb-related) or abstract nouns, decide which of those might be readily convertible to other parts of speech, or perhaps even left out. If your goal, besides providing an accurate rendition of the original, is to help the reader by "humanizing" the text, you could opt for an active verb with a personal subject, or even a "body verb" if the context warrants it. Take this passage for example:

> Необходимо нацелить <u>управление</u> на <u>повышение</u> <u>эффективности</u> и качества, <u>ускорение</u> НТП, <u>развитие</u> <u>заинтересованности</u> работников в результате труда в каждом звене.

An unfortunate, but fairly typical, attempt at translation might look like this:

> It is necessary to direct the management towards raising efficiency and quality, accelerating scientific and technical progress, and developing the interest of workers in the results of labor in every sector.

The result is a typically flawed translation of a typically flawed text, displaying every attention-loser the author and the translator could muster in just two lines. In addition to the use of what must have been the first dictionary entry for many of the words, there is the tin ear of both author and translator to the proliferation of -ание and -ение process nouns and -ность abstractions. A variant translation that avoids some of these pitfalls and attempts to salvage the sense does a better job:

> Economic managers must set their sights on improving efficiency and upgrading the quality of their product, speeding technological advance and creating better incentives for workers in every sector.

CHAPTER 6

CORRECTNESS – GRAMMAR AND USAGE IN ENGLISH

GRAMMAR – THE ROAD FROM RUSSIAN TO ENGLISH

As an English speaker, you may not always grasp the fine points of the original Russian, or be able to handle the complexities of the grammar. Reviewing and comparing grammar for equivalents and non-equivalents is always useful, and makes for a deeper understanding of both languages.

The norms of English grammar will be discussed here only where they directly impact on mistakes in translation, or when the choice of one option over another might affect the content or the style of the translation. Both the problems and the solutions arise out of the fundamental differences between Russian and English. Each language is rich in its own resources, but even apparent similarities can sometimes cause trouble.

Catching mistakes during translation depends to a great extent on the attention the translator pays to the grammar of the original, with special care reserved for case endings, prepositions, verb tenses (including tense jumps) and verb aspects, as well as punctuation, especially commas, quote marks and dashes, and also capitalization.

It is important to recognize the different approaches to correct usage in the two languages. In addition to grammar, elements here include proper nouns, numbers, and collocations: "What would go with that word in English?" It might well not be the same combination as in Russian.

Back to grammar, pure and simple. Suppose you are not sure what preposition to use in English—try an attributive construction instead. And don't be overly influenced by an attractive Russian collocation. Remember, in the target language, usage is king!

Other grammar points to check in a translation include agreement between subject and verb, because careless mistakes can creep in when these are widely separated. A decision must be made on which article to use in English—not an impossible task, even though this category does not exist in Russian. The original often contains other indications, especially the relationship between the "setting" (theme) and the "focus" (rheme) of the sentence, as well as case endings and the position of a word in the sentence. For example, the case of a noun combined with a verb in one aspect or another provides information regarding use of the article in English:

необходимо <u>пить</u> <u>воду</u> в течение дня

Here the copulative/link verb is understood, though необходимо should not always be rendered as "*it is necessary.*" A better idea is to use the imperative of the principal verb:

<u>Drink water throughout the day</u>
but
выпей <u>воды</u> = <u>drink some water</u>
выпей <u>воду</u> = <u>drink (up) the water</u>
<u>отпей воды</u>/<u>водички</u> = drink a little (bit); just take a sip

Or in an example commonly used in the classroom, the difference is between мальчик вошёл в комнату = "*the boy came into the room*" (a boy already known) and вошёл в комнату мальчик which could mean either "<u>*a*</u> boy" or "<u>*the*</u> boy," depending on the context, i.e., whether this is a surprise visit or if either the only boy around is expected, or the only girl.

Another example signaling the need for an article in a back reference in the text:

а в <u>данный</u> момент   at <u>the</u> moment

Accepted word order for pairs of nouns/pronouns/adverbs:
Some members of a commonly used pair or series are interchangeable. Others "sound wrong" if not in the customary order. Some correspond to the usual order in Russian:

соль и перец	salt and pepper
брат и сестра	brother and sister
раз или два	once or twice
муж и жена	man/husband and wife; he and I
взад и вперёд	to and fro

Other pairs need to be restructured in English:

я и он / и он и я	he and I; both he and I
я и моя жена	my wife and I
мы с ним	he and I; we

Verb tenses and aspects

Tenses and aspects can be tricky, too, especially with the treacherous verbs of motion and variations in certain other verbs. What is the difference in usage, for example, between встаньте, вставайте, становитесь, встать!, and встали!? Or take сядьте, садитесь, присаживайтесь, and сели; or say, идем and пошли? The answer is often found in the context, which can guide you in your translation. If the action in the imperative above is being required politely, as in встаньте, it could be translated as: "*Stand over here*" (accompanied by a gesture), or "*Will/Would you please stand?*" to a person in the audience or in a court of law, or even "*Oh, do get up!*" to someone perhaps standing on his knees in supplication. With вставайте, the action required is probably expected as part of, say, an exercise routine. Although вставайте or вставай would be heard in the morning, as "*time to get up!*" More information usually accompanies становитесь, say, становитесь в ряд. Встать! is a sergeant's or policeman's barked command, while встали! sounds like the peremptory tone used to address a class in school or at a gym, similar to the English "*Up!*" A similar use is to be seen in other verbs, such as: пошли, поехали, or сели. Do not confuse this imperative form with a verb in the past tense, as in:

> Они сегодня встали рано, не было и шести (часов).
> They were/got up early today—it wasn't even six.

Verb tenses may lead to a series of problems. They can also help solve some of them. Take the following sentence:

> Он еще раз <u>подчеркнул</u>, что позиция Великобритании <u>ни в коей мере</u> не <u>меняется</u>.
> He <u>repeated</u> that Britain's stand had not, <u>and would not</u> change.

The present-tense меняется is creatively interpreted using two other verb forms for emphasis. To avoid subjecting the Western reader to the same mistake as is evident in the Russian original, the typically overused подчеркнул instead of сказал becomes redundant when еще раз is converted into a verb. And in texts where "*said*" is not strong enough, other possible renderings of подчеркивать are "*maintain, hold, assert, insist, declare*"—and one need only consult a thesaurus to find plenty more.

The aspect of certain verbs is expressed through internal changes, while with others a prefix does the job. In many cases, particularly if the verb refers to an attempted action, use *"try to do,"* or some contextually appropriate expression:

решать / решить
Надо решать эту проблему уже сейчас. (*to address*)
We must *get to work on* / *deal with* / *try to resolve* this problem right away.
  (*contextual*)

В лаборатории много месяцев решали проблему несвоевременного
  свертывания крови.
The lab worked for many months on the problem of delayed coagulation.
  (*contextual*)

Необходимо окончательно решить этот вопрос.
We must settle/resolve this problem once and for all.
We must find the solution/answer to this problem once and for all.

уговаривать / уговорить
Я долго его уговаривал.
I tried and tried to talk him into it.
I tried and tried to convince him to do it.
I tried to talk him into doing it.
I tried to get him to do it.
I kept arguing with him to do it.
I argued for/with him to do it.
I tried to persuade him to do it.

Наконец уговорил.
And he finally agreed.; At last I succeeded.; At last I persuaded him.
(*conversive, logical development*)

добиваться / добиться
Три месяца я добивался встречи с начальником.
For three months I tried to get an appointment with the director.

Я добивался того, чтобы они меня перевели в другой отдел.
What I wanted was to be transferred to another department.
I tried to get them to transfer me.

В конце концов добился того, что меня просто уволили.
I ended up (just) getting fired.
In the end, I simply got (myself) fired.

поступать/ поступить (apply/try to get in)
Девушка не раз поступала в институт, но безуспешно.
The girl had *applied to / tried out for* college more than once, but—no luck!

Наконец поступила.
At last she *was accepted / succeeded / made it.*

сдавать / сдать
Я совсем не готова сдавать экзамен!
I'm not nearly ready to take that exam!

Ура! Самый трудный экзамен сдала, да еще на тройку!
Hey! I passed the hardest one, with a C – imagine!

Other verb aspects are expressed through prefixes:

пугать / испугать(-ся) / напугать
Нас <u>пугали</u> банкротством.
They <u>kept talking about</u> bankruptcy. (*implication*)
Bankruptcy was the big <u>bogey</u>. (*conversive and contextual*)

Малую фирму <u>пугали</u> полным уничтожением.
The smaller firm <u>was told</u> they would be (totally) destroyed. (*generalization*)

Мы испугались, думали, (что) наша компания будет съедена
  Корпорацией.
We were afraid we'd be swallowed up by the Big One.

Ой, как ты меня напугал! (*tone of voice depending on context*)
Oof! You startled me! (*literal*)
Oh, you really scared me, didn't you! (*sarcastic*)

Lastly, aspect can be expressed via a different verb altogether:

плутать / заблудиться / блуждать / бродить
Наконец мы поняли, что совсем заблудились.
At last it got to us—we were lost.

Плутали мы битый час пока не <u>вышли</u> на дорогу.
We wandered around a full hour before <u>stumbling</u> onto the road.
(*Note the specific translation/tactic of "concretization," and also how the
  Russian negative becomes an English affirmative.*)

Бродить по аллеям было приятно, а они забрели в какие-то совершенно
  незнакомые дебри.
Strolling down the tree-lined lanes was pleasant, but they got off and onto
  some totally unfamiliar territory.

Particles, connectors and conjunctions

Finding the right way to connect sentences, or parts of the same sentence, can b⸱
difficult in any language. Translating them can be even harder, and Russian con⸱
tains many connectors and transitional elements, some of which need no trans⸱
lation at all.

Transitional elements include, but are not confined to, conjunctions and cer⸱
tain other lexical choices, because syntax could also play a part if you decide t⸱
rearrange the components. Such words should be translated if needed in Englisŀ
dispensed with if superfluous, added where necessary. Prepositions or phrase⸱
that help arrange a sentence in the proper order, also conjunctions and particles
can all play an organizational or transitional role. Do not allow the lack of a tran⸱
sition to cause a bump in the road for the reader.

However, do not translate or site Russian transitions/conjunctions automati⸱
cally. Be particularly wary of так, таким образом, and же, especially becaus⸱
же has several functions, to be seen in different contexts. One function denote⸱
contrast, as in "Я—за, он (же) против" (же here needs no translation). Anothe⸱
function adds emphasis to what is probably a repeated call for help: "Помогит⸱
же! Тут я, тут!" "*Help! Help! I'm (over) here!*" The repetition reinforces th⸱
effect in both languages. Or take "Он же брат тебе, а не кто-нибудь!" In thi⸱
example, the же is rendered not by a word but by switching the two parts of th⸱
sentence around, so as to place the key word in the key end position: "*He's no⸱
just anybody – he's your brother*," although placing "*not just anybody*" or "*afte⸱
all*" at the end might fit the bill, too. In still another example, the же expresse⸱
the idea of sameness: "В то же (самое) время." Yet that expression also has an⸱
other meaning, when it denotes contrast:

"В то же время, учтите, есть и другое мнение."
"However, there *is / happens to be* another opinion (as well)."

наряду с ...
... as well (*post-position*); together with ... (*pre-position*); as well as;
in addition to; besides (*post- or pre-position*)

... а также
does not always demand: as well as
more frequently, it is translated as just: "and" *or* "as was; as were; as did
so-and-so", *etc.*

Тем временем...
in the meantime; meanwhile; at this same time

Так, ...
as a connector with, or transition from, the previous sentence:
So ...; Then ...; Thus ...; Therefore ... (*or omit*)
For instance ...; For example ... (*or insert this phrase further along in the sentence*)

Тут все ясно.
No question on <u>that</u> count.
(*back reference, inverted order and antonymic translation*)

Так же сделали и мы.
That's what we did(, too).
We did the (very) same thing.

А в том, что касается занятости, как быть научным работникам?
But then with / *As for* / *However, with* the job situation we have today, what about the scientists/researchers/lab workers? (What will it be like for them?; What are they to do?; How will they survive/cope?)

... такие как / в том числе ...
... such as; including (*or omit*)

в этом плане
in this regard; in context; speaking of; a propos of that

In a different context, however:

... ну, а в таком плане ... тогда конечно ...
but with a scenario like that, ... then of course ...

надо/следует отметить
interestingly; for instance; for example; take ...

таким образом
thus; so; then; this means (*or omit*)

что касается самого президента, ...
(*as for* / *but*) the president (himself) ...

зато сам президент
The president (on the other hand,) (*or omit*)

зато у меня есть ...
instead (*compensation*)/but what I do have (*contrast*) (on the other hand, I have ...)

причем/при этом
(*lexical*) and; what is more; moreover; besides (*pre- or post-position*); in
addition; although (*depending on the context*)
(*syntactic*) *change the second verb to a participle depending on the sense or
omit the connector*

… пытаясь <u>при этом</u> представить себя блюстителем интересов народа
… pretending to protect *people's interests / the people*
… pretending to be the champion of *people's interests / the people*

… <u>при этом</u> делая вид, что это ее обидели, а не она обидчица/обидела.
… trying to make it look as if she was the victim, *(and) not / instead of* the
abuser

<u>Но</u> что <u>из этого следует?</u> Вывод о <u>невозможности</u> разоружения, как
(это) утверждают некоторые политики и на Западе, и в Китае?
What <u>then</u> is the <u>conclusion</u>? That disarmament is impossible, as some
policymakers in the West and in China *insist / have been saying*?

Fillers

These extra words or syllables, though they may provide no substantially new
information, are sometimes needed for correct grammar or usage in Russian, or
may be inserted for balance, end weight, or as a formal requirement. In English
use them, too, when necessary. The extra words here are inserted for better
flow—in both languages:

В этот раз он <u>видимо успел</u> причесаться, побриться.
or in a variant:
… появился причесанный, чисто выбритый.
This time he <u>arrived</u> with <u>his hair neatly</u> combed, <u>his face</u> clean shaven.
This time he arrived clean shaven, his hair neatly combed.
This time he must have had time to shave and comb his hair.

Interjections

Sometimes coupled with another emotional word or words, or an accompanying
sentence with inverted word order, interjections tend to intensify the emotion being
expressed. Translating them necessitates a holistic approach, grasping the entire
thought to express it as a whole, rather than translating the interjection separately
from the other words in the sentence. Besides, just "translation" may not be enough;
some form of compensation may be required. And although dictionaries afford a
modicum of help by providing collocations, not all interjections are given in standard dictionaries, nor can every case of usage be covered.

One of the most versatile of interjections, **ну** can express a variety of feelings, ranging from the tentative *"er"* or *"um"* (indicating hesitation):

Ну, пошел я, пожалуй.
So/Well/Um, I guess I'll be on my way.

Ну, не знаю, идти мне? нет?
Oh, I don't know … should I go? … Or not?

to an indignant reaction to perceived injustice:

Ну, <u>что</u> это такое! Как можно?
What is this anyway?
What's going on! How could you?
How can they do that?

Depending on context and intonation, this interjection can express amazement or disapproval:

Ну и ну!
Imagine!; Wow!; Well, well!; What a revolting development!

This in addition to the classic stand-alone "Ну?" or perhaps "Ну, что? " translated as "*So?*" that expects a prompt reply. Extended somewhat, it has yet another function:

"Ну и что (из этого)?"
"So what (of it)?"

Other interjections suggest various sounds:

Уф! Ну, я и устала!
Whew/Boy, am I tired/beat/pooped!

Фу! Чем это тут так пахнет/воняет?
Hey!/Phew! What's that smell/stink?

Фу! Не так! … Не сотню, а тысячу. Да не выиграл, а проиграл … И не он, а ты!
No, hey! / That's not it! / That's wrong! / That's not what I wanted to say! It wasn't a hundred (rubles), it was a thousand. And he didn't win, he lost. Did I say he? I meant you!

The example above is only a joke, with the speaker feigning annoyance at his own absentmindedness. More common is the chagrin, even vexation with oneself, that can be seen in someone's real frustration at not getting the name of the person right (here, the family member he needs):

Наташа! Фу — Сережа! Да фу-ты — Ваня!
Hey, Natasha! ... No, I mean Sergei! ... What's the matter with me? — Vanya!

The example below expresses profound indignation and an attempt to comfort someone by urging him/her to send "them" to wherever they belong and forget the whole thing:

Тьфу-ты, плюнь!; Плевать!; Да плюнь ты!; Да ну их!; Черт с ними!
Hey, forget it! They're not worth it!; Damn them all anyway!; To hell with them!
(*Clearly, any reference to "spitting" in the translation is out of the question, or at least unnecessary. But different cultures have different ways of expressing themselves, both verbally and non-verbally.*)

Вот так так!; Вот тебе/те (и) на!
Well!; Wow!; Hm!; Hah!
(*instead of the dated: "a pretty pass" or "a fine kettle of fish," this expresses surprise or consternation; after all, Russians no longer say* "Вот тебе, бабушка, и Юрьев день!" *nor do English speakers say, "That's a fine how d'ye do."*)

Contextually, these could be rendered as:

Didn't expect that!; What's that supposed to mean?; Revolting development!; Now what?

Сделай(-ка), а?
Aw, do it, okay?; ... you will? (*suggests a coaxing intonation*)

Ой, извините, я нечаянно!
Oh, sorry! I didn't mean to!

Ой-ой-ой!
Uh-oh!; oops!; oh, wow!; oh, gosh!; oh, my goodness!
(*Expresses various degrees of surprise, dismay, or even an onlooker's comment concerning someone else's trouble.*)

A skeptical "Ой ли?" however, expresses disbelief in a more intense way than the similar "так ли?" Contextually, it could be translated as: "*Are you quite sure?*" or "*Oh really?*" or "*Is that right?*" or in a more informal context: "*Yeah, right!*"

Ай-ай-ай! Tsk-tsk!
usually mild/ironical disapproval, but in certain contexts, can express real dismay: Oh, no!

Да ты что?
What do you mean!; What are you doing?; Are you crazy?

Да что это такое?
What is this anyway?; What's going on?; What's happening to me/him/you?

wo synonyms together are sometimes used in Russian and in English: choose
•ne or use both, but pause first and consider. Try to judge the author's intention,
nd also see which sounds better. Sometimes two words in English can be used
ɔ put across one in the original Russian, here also with inversion carried over
rom the Russian syntax to provide a transition from the previous sentence:

> По другому <u>оригинальна</u>/самобытна/своеобразна деревянная
> архитектура Сибири.
> <u>Unusual and interesting</u> in a different way is the wooden architecture of
> Siberia.

he emotional use of two synonyms together has an analogy in "freedom and
iberty," but you need not always translate both:

> … вызывает <u>гнев и возмущение</u>
> … <u>angers</u>; … provokes <u>outrage</u>

NAMES AND NUMBERS – GETTING THEM RIGHT

Russian and foreign names

Russian names should be verified to comply with established usage and spelling
n the U.S. Well-known Russian names that have long been seen in English texts,
vithout reference to the rules of phonetic transcription, should continue to appear
n the form most familiar to the English reader:

Петр Первый	Peter the Great (*neither* Piotr I *nor* Peter the First)
Рахманинов	*usually*: Rachmaninov *or* Rakhmaninov *but no problem with*: Rachmaninoff
Чайковский	Tchaikovsky *or even the old German spelling*: Tschaikowski *not the transliterated*: Chaikovskii
Шаляпин	Chaliapin/-e (*never* Shalyapin).

Be extra careful of the Russian spelling of foreign names and names of organi
zations, companies, etc. in the original text. These are sometimes spelled pho
netically in Russian. Check foreign names on the Internet. Don't take spelling
for granted. And don't just transliterate unless no information is available to the
contrary.

Numerical problems

Generally, metric measures should be changed to the English equivalent, with
some exceptions:

гектары
acres *or* square miles, *other metric measures, except in scientific or
technical texts*

10 килограмм
*the plural ending is often left off, as are case endings, while "kilo" obviates
the need for any ending at all*

15-20 тысяч лет назад эта местность была покрыта водой. Невероятно,
но так.
Fifteen to twenty thousand years ago, this land was covered with water.
Unbelievable, but true.
Can you believe that 15,000-20,000 years ago, this land was covered with
water?
(*Such liberties can be taken in a popular text to enliven the proceedings.*)

70%/процентов компьютерного парка не было использовано.
Seventy percent of computer stocks available were not being used.
Seventy percent of the computers they had available were not being used.

Since in English a sentence cannot start with a figure, either spell out the number
in translation, as in the above examples, or relocate it in the translation, as in:

Of the computers available, 70 percent were not being used.

Считают, что понадобится месяцев восемь / 8 месяцев на (проведение)
консультаций / для консультаций (*invert or not depending on degree of
certainty*)
(Some) Eight months are expected to be needed for (the) consultations.
Consultations are expected to take about eight months.

Russian style for writing dates and times differs from the forms common in the
U.S. Here are a few reminders:

Dates

13.XII.2004	12/13/04 *or* 12/13/2004
13 декабря 2004 г.	December 13, 2004

Time of day

18.30	6:30 p.m.
половина/пол седьмого вечера	half past six (in the evening)
03.00	3:00 a.m.
три часа ночи/утра	three o'clock in the morning
15.00	3:00 p.m.
три часа дня	three o'clock in the afternoon
14.40;	2:40 p.m.;
без двадцати (минут) три (дня) пополудни	twenty (minutes) to/of//before three (in the afternoon)

(*One would be hard-pressed to find* "пополудни" "*afternoon*" *in a Russian text or conversation today, though it still exists in some dictionaries, so use it only in a "period" setting.*)

13.15	1:15 p.m.
15 минут/четверть второго (дня)	a quarter past one (p.m.)

Other examples involving numbers:

На долю этой страны приходится половина всей добычи цинка в мире
confusing: This country's share of the zinc produced in the world amounts
to/equals/is 50 percent.
clearer: This country produces half of the world's zinc.

This, of course, does not apply to any other, non-numerical meaning of доля:

Там доля женщины незавидна.
A woman's life there is not a happy one.

A scientific text does not need radical changes to be more readable:

К первой зоне <u>относится</u> подповерхностный слой до <u>глубины</u> 300-600 м.
The *first zone / top layer* is measured from the surface (down) to a depth of
300-600 meters.

For a more popular re-do, however, besides the changes in syntax, convert from the metric to the English system, and approximate the numbers, as in:

> The first zone <u>lies</u> between the surface and about 1,000 to 2,000 feet <u>down</u>.

Because of the confusion experienced by many translators trained in the literary arts rather than the mathematical arts, someone in Moscow put together a Russian translation table, popularly known as "**Разы**," which provides indications for dealing with difficulties in translating texts involving a quantity: "*so many times less than it was before, or than something else.*" There was no trouble if it was more, or if a concrete figure was provided, rather the number of times less. Here are a few paraphrased examples:

> Это в полтора раза меньше, чем раньше думали.
> That is one-third or some 30 percent less than earlier thought.
> *or*
> ... <u>в</u> 1,5 раза меньше (в полтора раза) меньше
> ... 30 percent less, or (down to) two-thirds
> (*Remember that the decimal point, a comma in Russian, is a period in English.*)

... <u>в</u> три раза; раза три меньше	... down to (about) a third
... <u>в</u> два раза меньше	... half as much
... в два раза больше	... twice as much

But with <u>на</u>, the calculation is so much simpler:

> <u>на</u> 150 литров меньше/больше
> 150 liters less/more
>
> <u>на</u> 100 километров дальше/ближе
> a hundred kilometers farther/closer

PUNCTUATION – FOCUSING THE ATTENTION

Rules for the proper use of punctuation in Russian lie on the border between grammar and usage. Some act as road signs; others provide emphasis or commentary. Punctuation in Russian differs from English in several ways:

The comma

1. In Russian a comma is required before a subordinate clause, with or without что; no comma is used in English.

> Он считает, что ты ошиблась.
> He thinks (that) you are mistaken.
>
> Мы точно не знаем, когда поедем.
> We're not (exactly) sure when we start out.

2. A comma can be used in Russian where English requires a period (otherwise there is a run-on sentence, which would be incorrect in English). With a run-on sentence in Russian, translate as a new sentence or combine as a participial phrase, a coordinate or subordinate clause, or an absolute construction:

> Ира пошла по одной улице, Степан пошел по другой.
> Irina went up one street. Stepan went up another.
> Irina went up one street, while Stepan went up another.
> Irina went up one street, Stepan going up another.
> Irina went up one street, Stepan up another.

The comma that is required before an identifying word in Russian should not appear in the English translation:

> Мы, русские, так не говорим/ не так бы сказали (cf ... так (никогда) бы не сказали ...)
> We Russians would not put it like that.
> (*This implies a quibble regarding form—is it grammatically correct?, or modality—does it put across the tone?*)
> We Russians would never say (a thing like) that.
> (*Here the <u>substance</u> is emphatically at issue. In both cases, English omits the comma.*)

The "ambiguous comma" poses yet another problem. The translator sometimes has to decide whether two related words on either side of a Russian comma are far enough apart in meaning (in the Russian) to warrant an "*and*" instead of that comma (in English) in order to avoid misunderstanding, or whether they are close synonyms and meant to be standing in apposition. In the latter case, the English will require a different conjunction or explanatory words for clarity. Or simply reset the author's idea in your own words.

Девочка любила всякие бантики, финтифлюшки.
The little girl liked to have bows <u>in her hair</u> and <u>all sorts of</u> frills.

Extra words are inserted for clarity, more definitely separating the meaning of the *"bows"* and the *"frills."*

The original Russian sentence below includes a number of potential (and very common) problems. The solutions depend on the context in which they might appear, with a register/style level that varies with each translation. All these solutions interpret администрирование and произвол as appositives.

Его <u>обвиняли</u> в <u>грубом</u> администрировании, <u>произволе</u> <u>в его</u> <u>отношениях с</u> подчиненными / <u>по отношению к</u> подчиненным.
The staff complained of his authoritarian methods.
He was accused of high-handed treatment of his subordinates.
There were reports about the arbitrary procedures he introduced in the office.
With him it was always "rule by injunction/fiat."
He liked to throw his weight around.

Below, the use of снимает reinforces the idea of разрешает in the original, while *"not at all"* acts as reinforcement in the translation, and reflects both полностью and снимает.

Но это не означает, что наше общество полностью <u>разрешает</u> эти проблемы, <u>снимает</u> их.
That does not mean that our society has resolved these problems, <u>not at all</u>.

Finally, take the classic case of the misplaced comma—in the Russian. Literally a matter of life and death. Which will it be then, life … or death?—The comma will decide.

Помиловать, нельзя казнить!   Pardon (him). Do not execute!

Помиловать нельзя, казнить!   Pardon impossible. Execute!

Question marks and exclamation points

Russian sometimes uses two or even three exclamation marks to make a point, usage not acceptable in English. A question mark followed by an exclamation point, "Как же так?!", seldom works in English. The same goes for a question mark or exclamation point in parentheses, (?) (!), and particularly the two together, (?!). These are generally frowned upon as outdated, so limit your use. Instead, try to express the author's emotion (puzzlement, indignation) through careful word choice.

The exclamation point still often used in the salutation of a Russian letter becomes a comma in translation:

Дорогие мои Муся и Леня!   Dear Musya and Leo,

The colon

Be alert to another distinction between Russian and English punctuation. A colon in Russian may be used after an independent clause to introduce a list of particulars or a subordinate clause, often one that needs to be translated into English by "*because*" or "*that*." Otherwise write a separate sentence.

Учителя счастливы: пять часов дети провели на школьном дворе.
The teachers were happy <u>because</u> the children spent five hours out in the schoolyard.

А может быть, было другое объяснение: он Вас не избегал, он просто был занят!
Maybe there is another explanation, that he wasn't avoiding you – he was just busy!

The dash

A dash in the Russian may be purely grammatical (a substitute for a form of "*to be*"):

Вы—наше будущее!
You are our future!

Or it can be used instead of quotation marks in dialogue, whereas English uses only quotation marks.

—Эй, / А ну-ка, парень, пойди(-ка) сюда!—
"Hey, (you,) young fellow, come over here!"

—А что, дяденька, чего вам нужно?—
"What's the problem, (Pop)?"; "What's up?"; "What's the trouble?"

For other uses of the dash, perhaps for effect—to call attention to a "parenthetical" phrase like this one—use your own judgment. Which means don't go overboard! The dash can be addictive.

Quotation marks

Among other uses that differ between Russian and English, quotation marks in a translation are a frequent offender, requiring careful attention from the translator. A quotation that takes the form of a cleft sentence, where the speaker is identified in an insert ("*said so-and-so*") is different in Russian than in English, so the translator must use caution. Here are the two types of quotes in Russian, with only one option in English:

> – Нет, – сказала она, – не надо.
> "Нет, – сказала она, – не надо".
> "No," she said, "don't do it."; "let's not"; "I don't need it." (*as per context*)

> "Я ухожу, – сказала Анна, хотя еще рано".
> "I am leaving," said Anna, "even though it's early."

Note that while in American English end punctuation goes inside the quotation marks, in Russian the quotation mark precedes it.

Ambiguous quotation marks

Apart from the quotation marks we all know the use of, such as the direct quote, this form of punctuation can be ambiguous, leaving the Russian author's intention hanging in the air.

1. Does his use of quotation marks indicate his disapproval of the way a word has been used by others, thereby indicating his own skepticism? (cf. "*so-called*"…)?

   > Он обратил внимание на наши "ошибки", якобы допущенные во время суда.
   > He called attention to what he insisted were our mistakes.
   > He called attention to the mistakes we ostensibly made during the trial.
   > (*The quotation marks in Russian are reflected in the choice of words in the translation, although quotation marks in English need not be ruled out.*)

2. Is he showing that he knows that the word is slang or non-standard?

   > Они вовсю «пиарят» свой товар.
   > They are busily promoting their product.
   > (*The author's quotation marks need not be reflected in the translation. Note the slightly pejorative tone of the original, interpreted here as "busily," which would serve the same purpose.*)

If the author is not being sarcastic or disapproving, but merely calling attention to what he believes to be an unfamiliar word, it is better not to use the quotation marks, or use them with an unobtrusive explanation of his intention.

If the Russian has quotation marks or <u>так называемый</u>, the translation could use "*as it is known here*" or "*as we call it.*"

> так называемая болезнь Боткина
> Hepatitis A, or "Botkin's disease" [*with or without quotation marks*] as it was known to doctors in Russia

> так называемый эффект Доплера
> the Doppler effect (as it is called)

If a textbook is introducing a new term or concept, and words of explanation stand in apposition, the definite article may be enough.

Quotation marks are used around some titles in Russian but not commonly used in English: names of companies, books, plays, operas, musicals, ballets, periodical publications, etc.

An important word of caution: Quotes translated from the English (an English speaker or writer), when inserted into a Russian text, **must** be converted into indirect speech or a modified quote (<u>without</u> the quotation marks). In other words, you cannot translate the translated words back into English, not if you use quotation marks. Only if you find that very quotation in the original English (by looking it up on the Internet, etc.) can you insert it in your translation in quotes.

Creative punctuation and visual arrangement

This also includes capitalization, italics, bolding, underlining as they can focus attention and ease the reader's lot.

> exclamation point
> question mark
> quotation marks (*direct quote, new word, unusual usage, irony, "so-called"*)
> parentheses
> dash
> ellipsis (*the three dots that in addition to an omission can also signify a pregnant pause*)

> > А сюрпризом был десерт – мороженое домашнего изготовления!
> > The surprise ending was (actually) … homemade ice cream!
> > (*The context refers to a "surprise" that the diner was told to expect, plus the claim that modern housewives are always looking for table-ready shortcuts.*)

1. Make the most of the comma, inserting one where there would be a natural pause, leaving out a comma where it makes for too many pauses, inhibiting the flow of your English sentence. (The reader won't be too finicky about the "rules," but see the *Los Angeles Times Style Book* for more recommendations.)
2. Use bullets or numbers to separate points in the text (if your publisher allows it).
3. Indent where this helps, highlight the items needed, e.g., examples or illustrations.
4. Be abstemious with underlining and italics, but not a teetotaler.
5. A dash or two is an excellent way to make a component stand out, but again, don't overdo.
6. Go easy on the exclamation points, even if your author uses them.

Register – a suitable setting

Sometimes a translation is lexically and grammatically correct, and yet something just "doesn't sound right." By and large, the problem is one of register, finding the correct tone and stylistic level. Is the text a formal, official one? Literary? Scientific? Informal? This is one of the hardest elements to deal with in translation, because the boundaries between styles are so vague and undefined.

Formal or informal?

Your decision should at least partly depend on the prospective reader: does he expect an official or scholarly style, or would he find it easier to read through a more popular text? Take the way an advertisement ends with directions on how (and how fast) the TV viewer or Internet browser can/should/must contact the sponsor or spamster, as the case may be:

> Со всеми вопросами обращаться по ..... @ ....
> (*The @, the symbol for "at," is usually referred to as* собака *in informal Russian.*)

In a text where the Russian is less formal:

> Вопросы есть? Обращайтесь к нам на наш сайт ... www. ...
> Any questions? Visit us online at ... www. ...

Translators often mistakenly believe that the functional style level/register and general tone of the original must be reproduced in English, regardless of the comfort level of the average Western reader. For example, if an official speech or a newspaper editorial is couched in the terminology and syntax of elevated rhetoric in the Russian, then no word of colloquial English should be allowed to creep into the translation. The same would apparently apply to other texts, such as scientific or technical ones. Yet an important pragmatic consideration ought to be kept in mind when translating such a text: can the reader grasp the meaning and read through the entire text without undue difficulty? Or will he get bogged down in unfamiliar terms and structures? If changing terminology is impractical or undesirable, then syntactic changes at least can be introduced to speed his progress through the text.

Elevated rhetoric: where should it be converted to a lower register?

Take the following examples:

родина
country of origin; home (country); native country; the old country
(*This is probably non-emotive, although there may be a hint of nostalgia in the text, yet it would not call for a capital letter.*)

The example below is another illustration of an emotionally neutral use:

Он потом уехал обратно к себе на родину.
He later went home.
He later went back to his own country.

With Родина, however, the ritual capitalization in the Russian (when the word is applied to Russia itself) calls for a more emotive approach in English. But this should not be overdone—don't use "*Motherland/Fatherland*," unless the author is introducing a foreign factor (or actor). Absent such a condition, better use "*this nation*," "*our country*," "*(native) land*," or "*homeland*," so that the required elevated tone will be retained:

Наша Родина – превыше всего!
Our homeland comes first! [*cf.* … über alles]

The following is a step-by-step comparison of the translation of a phrase in descending order of "formality":

записавшиеся в список ораторов
those who have entered their names on the list of potential speakers
those who have expressed a desire to speak
those who indicated that they wanted to speak
(those) speakers on the list

Meanwhile, certain popular science translation techniques can be applied to strictly scientific texts or any other type that could benefit from a less formal style in translation:

> После <u>смерти</u> <u>остатки</u> организмов, <u>опускаясь вниз</u>, интенсивно
> <u>разлагаются</u> в подповерхностных водах.
> After an organism/individual <u>dies</u>, its remains <u>sink</u> and (soon) <u>disintegrate</u>
> (at a rapid rate) in the subsurface waters.

Here nouns and participles have been verbalized, a redundant adverb left out, and another converted by employing the professional's tactic of "logical development."

> В процессе разложения <u>затрачивается</u> огромное количество кислорода,
> <u>в результате чего</u> на этих глубинах <u>наблюдается</u> <u>пониженное</u>
> содержание кислорода, <u>так называемый</u> "слой кислородного
> минимализма".
> The process of decay <u>consumes</u> an enormous amount of oxygen, reducing
> its content at these depths to what is seen as a minimum.

Converting the reflexive verbs <u>затрачивается</u> and <u>наблюдается</u> to an active form makes it easier to access the sense; the rest of the sentence is simplified to its own "minimum."

"Learnèd" words / "long" words

"Learnèd" words are words the reader sees so seldom that he may need to consult a dictionary before he can understand them. In translation, try to steer clear of them:

> … все то, что <u>сопутствовало</u> / все факторы, <u>сопутствующие</u> росту
> человечества
> *Not*: mankind's <u>concomitants</u>
> *Better*: everything that has (inevitably) <u>accompanied</u> the development of
> mankind
> *or*
> everything that has <u>accompanied</u> mankind as we developed (over
> the millennia)

"Humanizing"

To make a translation more reader-friendly, it may be possible to employ certain tactics—lexical, syntactic, stylistic—but only if justified by the context or situation. A sensitive approach is key:

- convert abstract/process nouns to a finite verb, with personal agents as subject
- convert abstract/process nouns with a prop to finite verbs or any active form, including participles
- cut an abstract -ность noun to its core, changing the part of speech if necessary
- watch out for leftover –ание's and -ение's and deal with them forthwith
- move to a lighter register (colloquial or conversational version)

должны нести главную ответственность за ...
must be (held) chiefly responsible for ...

современность
modern times; today; in our day

необычайная задушевность и музыкальность творчества Н.
the soul and music of N's poetry

являются основным препятствием разрешения ...
or
(на пути) к разрешению проблемы
constitute/are the main obstacle to (finding) a solution (to the problem)

Регистрация делегатов проводится от/с 10 до 20 часов.
Delegates can register from 10 am to 8 pm.
Delegates will be registering from 10 am to 8 pm.

In addition, adjust the reference to time with added am or pm, except in a military or other specialized text.

Informal styles: colloquial, conversational, familiar

Translating dialogue or any text resembling a conversation can be exciting, challenging, and truly enjoyable. Here again, once the meaning of the individual words is clear, the main thing is to see through to the intention of the author, both in content and in tone. Compare the examples below. The first is spoken in polite, formal language, while the second style has a more relaxed, familiar tone, without getting slangy:

1. Не хотите ли перекусить?
   Would you care for *some lunch / something to eat*?

   Спасибо, не откажусь.
   Thanks, I *believe I would / won't say no.*

2. Есть хочешь?
   (Are) (you) hungry?
   How about a little something?
   Ready for a bite?

   Хочу. / Давай.
   I sure am.
   (Yes,) okay.
   Good, let's (go) eat.

Давай, incidentally, is a most versatile term, applicable in a request, an offer, o
a reply in the affirmative, e.g. "*okay*" or "*let's.*" And as давайте, it is suitable i
a more formal exchange:

Давайте еще раз обдумаем этот немаловажный вопрос.
   Хорошо/Согласен, давайте. С чего начнем?
Let's go over / Suppose we go over / Why don't we go over that point again.
   It's important. All right, let's. What do we start with?

CHAPTER 7

EDITING FOR CLARITY, EASE AND EFFECT

As a translator of written texts, you have a distinct advantage over your colleagues, the interpreters, be they simultaneous or even consecutive. You have time to look at least a few sentences ahead before you start the actual translation, and you also have (or should have) the luxury of time to edit your work for clarity, flow, and greater effect, and to hunt down typos and other errors. If you have a computer with a spell check and a grammar option, don't disable them. No matter how annoying their suggestions may be, you will one day be grateful to the person who invented them in the first place.

Try not to carry over the stylistic mistakes of the Russian into your translation:

> … испытывали <u>определенные</u> трудности в <u>определении</u> природы этого явления
> experienced *a certain degree of / some* difficulty determining the nature of the phenomenon
> had a hard time understanding what (exactly) was happening

Some wake-up calls are signals to watch out for before deciding whether to carry over a component into your translation, or else to modify, replace, or omit it altogether. Particularly widespread is the "prop-verb + process noun" combination that plagues so many texts.

Lexical

• all-purpose, "prop" verbs (e.g., осуществлять, проводить) plus a "process" noun:

> провести беседу
> give/have a talk (for/with)
> talk (to/with) (*verbalize*)
> <u>have</u> a talk (*about almost any conversation, even for educational purposes*)
> cf. <u>give</u> a talk (*not a conversation, this denotes a lecture, live before an audience or on TV*)

- verb-related "process nouns," including, though not confined to -ание and -ение suffixes (same as above)

- abstract nouns

Syntactic—balance, rhythm and flow: how to improve them?

- rearrange sentence structure to highlight important elements, relocating some that delay or interrupt progress to the "nub" of the sentence.

- condense a wordy sentence/paragraph to avoid verbosity in your translation and hold the reader's attention. A translated sentence that cannot otherwise be faulted, but is just too "busy" (with unnecessary words and even syllables) will tire any reader in time.

- spread out a densely packed sentence/paragraph, to provide more "air"

- see to it that structures within a sentence, e.g., lists, phrases, clauses, hold to a parallel scheme

Editing one's own translations (and occasionally other people's) is a very rewarding activity, though sometimes frustrating, too, when the right words refuse to appear on one's radar, or in any available dictionary (more on that later). Or perhaps the syntax or structure of the original stubbornly intrudes in the translation. The satisfaction of reading through a well-edited text is matched only by one that is well-written in the first place.

A recap then of the methods every good translator should have at his fingertips:

- See to it that your version makes sense and conforms to English usage, including collocations—what goes with what—and register (style level), and adequately reflects the author's attitude (favorable-unfavorable), whether directly (denotation) or by implication (connotation).

- Check proper names: personal, geographic, newspapers (on the Internet, etc.). Don't take spelling for granted. Some names have traditional forms and spelling in English, even though these may depart from the accepted systems of transliteration.

- For names of organizations or commercial firms, do your research. If no official translation exists, follow the rules for accurate and effective translation or transliteration. Do not use quotation marks for such names.

- Try several versions of word choice and syntax in your translation before finally making a decision. Do not follow Russian syntax slavishly. For instance, choose between different adjective forms, active or passive verbs, etc.

- Avoid "learnèd" words that force readers to go to the dictionary or risk misunderstanding. Substitute simpler ones, but beware of style-level misfits that are too colloquial or slangy for a given context.

- Identify abstract or process nouns, and where necessary turn them into finite verbs, supplying a subject from the context or your own store of knowledge, other parts of speech, or omitting where the meaning does not suffer.

- Identify intensifiers in both the Russian and your translation and gauge the required strength/expressiveness of the word they modify.

- Do the same for connectors/transitions between sentences, perhaps inserting as needed, or combining sentences, as with a participial construction, a subordinate clause, or even a simple "*and*."

- Eliminate verbosity by weeding out unhelpful repetition, and when omitting "prop" verbs adjust the grammar in the rest of the sentence. Cognates in the same sentence are annoying, a pronoun or other pro-form might help, but some repetition, used wisely, helps hold the text together and keep the reader's attention.

- Try to avoid long attributive phrases (or two or three) before a noun. Relocate, condensing if desirable. Consider changing their function in the sentence.

- Recast sentences to rid them of delays and unnecessary interruptions.

DICTIONARIES – IN PRINT AND ONLINE

Non-translators generally go to the dictionary when they need a definition, spelling, or pronunciation, rarely for usage. Absent the need for a specialized term, a translator usually starts with usage. So if a bilingual or monolingual dictionary has no indication of how a word should be used, in what context or collocation, it is of little benefit to him. The more details and combinations are given, the better. A bilingual dictionary (e.g., the *Russian-English Oxford*, or the Katzner dictionary, or Harper-Collins dictionary, or *Русско-Английский Словарь* Смирницкого [the Smirnitsky *Russian-English Dictionary*] published in Russia) besides providing an equivalent in another language, differs from a monolingual dictionary (a *Webster's* or *OED*, say) in other ways as well. A good resource for translators must cover more ground, including appropriate usage and combinations, technical level and age, and might even cover potential transformation, grammatical or contextual/pragmatic points, and also synonyms, like a thesaurus (e.g., the classic *Roget, Webster's New World Thesaurus*, or *The Complete Word*

Finder, a combination of dictionary and thesaurus, published jointly by Oxford and the *Reader's Digest*).

There are books of Russian idioms that explain meaning and provide usage, with examples from literature. One such book is the *Russian-English Dictionary of Idioms*, by Sophia Lubensky. You may also find a clue by consulting the Internet in English or Russian (Cyrillic), or by resorting to human help.

Online resources that have made their appearance in recent years are eminently useful in many ways, but the equivalents they provide must sometimes be taken with a grain of salt. *Rambler* has received kudos from a number of translators (mostly from English to Russian), but *Multitran* is probably the all-around favorite, with dozens of combinations arranged according to a variety of subjects. As with virtually any other dictionary or thesaurus, however, the translator has to pick and choose, bringing his own linguistic and practical life experience into the mix. In addition to the many specialized reference books available in print (including technical and legal, but also glossaries on practically any subject), other good online resources include *Context* and *Lingvo*.

Searching ... for what? (not a word, I hope)

Sometimes no dictionary entry seems to supply the exact word needed. But there are times when the word that one is seeking is simply unnecessary. The secret, once again, is in "the thought"—imagine the situation and translate the thought.

разворовали музейные ценности

Don't agonize over those ценности: it's not "*values*" (wrong context—that's something in your head or your heart), it's not "*valuables*" (more often applied to jewelry and personal belongings), nor even "*exhibits*" (they do belong in museums, true, but not in this sentence). The solution here is simpler—leave it out. It's "*looted the museums*."

CHAPTER 8

NOTES ON EVERYDAY RUSSIAN CULTURE

Translating "culture," i.e. cultural references, is one of the most difficult tasks facing the translator, and in a book of this limited size and scope can only be touched upon briefly. The following examples indicate the kinds of problems the translator faces, and various possibilities for rendering the реалии (features of Russian life) in English.

Sovietisms

"Sovietisms" that have survived into post-Soviet times can sometimes be found in a Russian-English dictionary, but it is important to distinguish those that are still taken seriously from those that, if used at all, now have an ironical tinge (at least when not describing life in the USSR in the past). Both categories include abbreviations and acronyms: Генсек (*Secretary General*), полпред *(Ambassador, or other diplomat plenipotentiary representing a country)*, Госсекретарь (*U.S. Secretary of State*), соцработкик (*social worker*), капремонт (*major repairs/remodeling*), госбезопасность *(national/state security)*, медсестра (*RN*), МИД or Министерство иностранных дел (*Foreign Ministry*). Then there are complete words, such as коллектив: "*the workers, workforce, staff, team,*" or specifically: "*company, factory, student body, teaching staff.*"

Words describing actual features of Soviet-era life: субботник, стахановец, соцсоревнование, колхоз, ударник, агитатор, and pompous-sounding phrases, such as широкие массы трудящихся, трудовой фронт, воспитывать нового человека, have pretty much disappeared from use by writers today (making life that much easier for the conscientious translator), but they are still listed in a number of dictionaries. Some equivalents appear just as they did in bygone days. Агитатор, in addition to "*campaigner*" and "*canvasser,*" is still translated just "*agitator.*" And агитация remains as "*propaganda work among the masses,*" although today (and in colloquial usage back then as well), "Не надо меня агитировать, все равно не пойду!" is closer to "*Don't bug me—I'm still not going!*" Among friends and colleagues, use of the "official" meaning was treated with skepticism, or repeated tongue in cheek. Don't forget that for агитпункт, meaning "*a local canvassing post*," someone once invented "*agitation station*." Yet though a few dictionaries still define ударник as "*shock worker*," this sort of worker has disappeared without a trace from most reference works, yielding his place to someone in a completely different category: "*percussionist*" or "*(So-and-so) on the drums.*"

трудовое воспитание
not: labor education
better: vocational class; occupational training class

молодые специалисты
recent college graduates (*often in an entry-level job*)
not: specialists; experts

привязывать к предприятию
not: to tie workers to their factory
but: to make it so that workers would *not leave / want to stay on*
(*officially* retention, *this paraphrase serves as an unobtrusive explanation*)

Ему советовали подлечиться в санатории.
It was recommended that he / He was told that he should go to a *rehab (clinic) / health resort* to *recover / get better* (before going back to work).
(*Remember that "sanitariums/sanatoria" in the West are medical facilities for patients recovering from serious illnesses, such as tuberculosis, while "санатории" in Russia rarely have that purpose, often being just an alternate vacation site with a doctor's referral, more like rehab combined with a medically supervised spa.*)

Музей был объявлен музеем-заповедником.
The museum was put under special government protection.

военный бизнес
those who make a business of war; the military-industrial complex

Variations on the theme of "*absences*," sanctioned and not:

прогул	AWOL from work or school
отгул	day off (*as compensation for overtime*)
"Я завтра гуляю."	"I'm off tomorrow." (*colloquial*)
выходной	(regular) day off; "the weekend" (*if plural*)
"Иди! Гуляй!"	"Go fly a kite!"; "Go jump in the lake!; "Scram!"; "Beat it!; "Get lost!" (*or a more up-to-date way of angrily telling someone to go away and leave one alone*)

завтрак/-ать	breakfast (*no longer* "lunch"; *but could be* "brunch")
второй завтрак	*akin to* "grand dejeuner" (*no longer in use*)
перекусить	lunch (*American style; usually not just a snack between meals*)
обед/-ать	dinner (*usually the main meal, eaten during the* "обеденный перерыв" – "*lunch break*," somewhere between 2 and 4 pm)
ужин/-ать	supper (*usually lighter than the midday meal, eaten between 7 and 9 pm, depending on working hours*)

In the first sentence below, note the context-specific words as more focused, instead of "*document*" and "*reflects.*" Incidentally, "политический" in Russian (say, "политический шаг" — "*a matter of policy*") does not always have the same meaning as "*political*" does in English, although in the example, thanks to the word общие, they do match up. Sometimes in the U.S., "*a political move*" or "*for political advantage*" would be understood as "в узко политических целях"; "*a political appointment*" would be rendered as "назначение по чисто политическим соображениям."

Документ отражает общие политические цели.
The agreement points to common political goals.

укрепить дисциплину
improve discipline/compliance (*use this if it is important to mitigate the effect of tighten/toughen/strengthen*)

активно вести пропаганду современного российского музыкального
   творчества
popularize / publicize / get people acquainted with modern Russian music (*to avoid the words* "*propaganda*" *and* "*art*" *in English if they do not match the situation*)

The Terminology of Education

A text on education requires the translator's special attention because the systems in Russia and the United States differ substantially.

Though детский сад looks like a calque of "*kindergarten,*" in reality it includes both a continuation of daycare and even part of the first grade in America if one takes into account the amount of learning that is expected there. Since первый класс begins at age six or seven (or even eight, if your birthday falls after the first day of school), some preparation is considered desirable, if not absolutely necessary. Incidentally, *"grade"* = класс in Russian, while "grade" in its other meaning of *"mark"* = отметка or оценка.

After the детский сад, начальная школа covers grades 1 to 4, middle school grades 5 to 9, and seniors in grades 10 to 11. The students in all the grades are located in the same building, called the средняя школа, though in separate sections. The word студент itself, unlike *"student"* in English, refers only to a college student, while аспирант is what we would call a graduate student. Meanwhile, the word for an elementary school student in Russian is ученик, while yet another term, учащийся, refers to either an elementary or a high school student.

If that weren't enough of a difference, when the старшеклассник (*high school senior*) graduates after completing eleven grades, not twelve, he gets an аттестат зрелости, not a diploma. But upon graduation from his/her институт or университет after five or six years of study, compared with our typical four, he finally does get a диплом, or what is known in the U.S. as a degree (BA or BS). The (ученая) степень in Russia would correspond to an American advanced degree, and here is where the disparity in terms, as well as content, differs the most. The кандидат (наук) actually is a doctoral candidate, but we rarely call him that; here he is an MS or MA. Доктор наук typically is considerably harder to achieve than the PhD, as anyone getting evaluated or certified abroad knows.

CHAPTER 9

Practice Texts

Converting a serious, even a technical text to a more popular ("human," not frivolous) style level for an easier read in translation is often possible. Following is a short sample text and suggested translation with analysis:

Общественное производство всегда бывает связано с преобразованием природы либо стихийным, хищническим, либо плановым, обуславливающим воспроизводство ресурсов, масштабы которого все увеличиваются.

В силу всего этого, изучение географической оболочки может быть успешным лишь при детальном познании влияния человеческого общества на природу, обусловленного способом производства.

Confusing: Social production is always connected with alteration of nature, either uncontrolled, ruthless or planned, conditioning reproduction of resources, the scale of which is constantly increasing, in view of all of which, the study of the earth's crust can be successful only with detailed study of the human effect on the environment, conditioned on the method of production.

Clear: Industry will always alter the environment, but this can be done either in an unregulated, even rapacious way or else properly regulated, stipulating that resources must be renewed on an ever-broadening scale. So that studying the environment can be meaningful only if there is also a detailed study of man's impact on his environment, and that depends on what production methods he employs.

Version 1 (itself unregulated and unplanned) is typical "translatese," faithful to the words, traitorous to the thought. It badly needs editing to put the idea across and make life easier for the reader.

In Version 2, общественное is dropped because "*social*" here would be a specialized Marxist term, out of place in a popular article on the environment. "*Production*" in English is a process and as such is not itself capable of action: for this reason "*industry*" is made the subject of the sentence because it can perform actions such as "*altering the environment.*" This change makes possible a direct, active verb without recourse to the combination "связано с преобразованием" (involving a process noun plus a vague, all-purpose verb as semi-operator, actually a prop).

The short six-word Russian element, либо стихийным, хищническим, либо плановым, is expanded to sixteen words in the English (counting the auxiliary verb and articles), so as to give the thought more space, and so lighten a densely packed text. Note the following elements which were added to achieve this more relaxed presentation:

- "*but*" graphically indicates the relationship between this part of the sentence and the preceding part.

- Географическая оболочка has apparently been used as a synonym for природа, but this sort of elegant variation to avoid repetition can be confusing, so it might be better simply repeat the word "*environment*" in the translation.

- "*This*" and "*is done,*" two pro-forms (substitute words) referring to "*altering,*" are chosen over other possibilities—"*this*" alone, "*done*" alone, or neither, beginning with just "*either...*" instead of the two adjectives that modify "преобразованием" in the Russian. We could have chosen to use single-word ("-ly") adverbs to modify our verb "*alters,*" but they are so awkward that we would gain little with this maneuver, so the two adverbial phrases are used instead, the added length notwithstanding.

- For "обуславливающим", a participle form of another blurry high-frequency verb, together with its abstract noun "воспроизводство," we have a clause that once again expands the structure. By doing this, we give the reader some needed breathing space. The fact that the Russian reflexive "увеличиваются" remains a passive (and a subjunctive at that) is justified because we can locate the phrase "*on ... scale*" in the advantageous final position in English.

- "Всего" is dropped because it does not refer to anything in the immediate context. Even translating the words "географической оболочки" would be needlessly pedantic in a text like this, so the simpler and more concrete "*environment*" is substituted.

- The "при" phrase and subsequent chain of fairly abstract nouns in the genitive case is replaced by a subordinate clause that exposes the core of the meaning and makes the construction personal. "При" plus an abstract should always be viewed with suspicion; even "при" with any noun should ring an alarm bell—there are so many meanings.

• Instead of "обусловленного", an unfortunate repletion in the Russian, and with a different meaning besides, we can once again make use of a "which" clause with its own object clause, bringing out the meaning painlessly and efficiently.

All in all, the additional wordage in the English is hardly felt, compensated for, as it is, by a reader-friendly humanization of the text.

Texts from published books and articles

For convenience, the selected excerpts are arranged with alternating original and translated paragraphs to bring them closer together, eliminating unnecessary page turning. Suggested procedure is to read all the paragraphs in the original Russian, skipping over the translation. Then, without consulting the English provided, translate the original, paragraph by paragraph, noting underlined words that indicate potential problems. After that, consult the translation provided, compare your work with that of the professional translator, and note agreement and disagreement.

From a text on Soviet history:

Послевоенный СССР всегда привлекал внимание специалистов и читателей, интересующихся прошлым Советского Союза. Победа советского народа в самой страшной войне в истории человечества стала звездным часом России XX века. Но вместе с тем, она стала и важным рубежом, обозначившим наступление новой эры – эпохи послевоенного развития. Эта эпоха вместила в себя многие судьбоносные для СССР события – смерть Сталина, хрущёвскую "оттепель" и определила векторы развития советского государства и коммунистической партии вплоть до их исчезновения с политической арены.

The Soviet Union in the postwar period has been a constant source of interest for anyone—historian or general reader—who wants to learn more about its past. The victory of the Soviet people in the most devastating war in history was twentieth-century Russia's finest hour, but it also signaled the advent of a new era, one of postwar development and momentous events, such as the death of Stalin and Khrushchev's "thaw," which determined how the Soviet state and the Communist Party would evolve right up to the moment they exited the political scene.

В советской <u>историографии</u> вплоть до конца 80-х годов <u>исторический отрезок</u> 1945-1964 годов <u>находился на периферии</u> исследовательского поиска. В отношении этих лет <u>советская историческая наука</u> ограничивалась лишь набором определённых идеологических штампов, навязанных "сверху", практически устранившись от <u>активной разработки</u> <u>данного </u>периода. В то же время на Западе <u>осуществлялось</u> <u>полнокровное</u> исследование этого важнейшего исторического этапа в жизни СССР. <u>Был создан</u> большой массив <u>литературы,</u> где анализировались <u>самые различные</u> стороны функционирования советской системы в послевоенный и хрущёвские периоды. Как известно, фактически вплоть до 90-х годов <u>труды</u> зарубежных исследователей <u>характеризовались</u> как <u>историческое</u> <u>фальсификаторство</u>. Их <u>подходы</u> и теории следовало "разоблачать".

Until the late 1980s, the subject of the first twenty postwar years (1945–1964) was fairly well <u>marginalized</u> by Soviet <u>historians</u>, who had to employ the ideological clichés imposed from above and refrain from any <u>in-depth analysis</u> of the period. Historians in the West, on the other hand, paid it more than adequate attention, <u>with</u> a large <u>body</u> of <u>work</u> examining the various aspects of the Soviet system in the first postwar years and under Khrushchev. But all through that time, Soviet <u>propaganda stigmatized</u> these <u>studies</u> as <u>"fraudulent" and "falsified,"</u> and declared that their <u>judgments</u> and theories had to be "exposed."

Отношение к работам западных советологов зависело от <u>степени приближенности</u> их выводов к <u>утвердившимся в советской историографии</u> оценкам исторических <u>явлений и событий</u>. Однако, <u>нам представляется</u>, что <u>вклад зарубежных исследователей в изучение рассматриваемого периода весьма ценен</u>. Многие наработки, сделанные советологами, явились серьезным подспорьем для <u>отечественных ученых</u> в 90-х годах, когда <u>началось</u> <u>переосмысление пройденного исторического пути,</u> <u>освобождение</u> от жесткой идеологической <u>зашоренности</u>. Вот почему сегодня <u>так необходимы</u> исследования, которые, <u>учитывая различное отношение к историческим фактам, событиям, явлениям</u> позволяли бы сделать более объективные, непредвзятые, <u>неполитизированные</u> выводы.

The attitude to Western sovietologists at that time depended on <u>how closely their views tallied</u> with evaluations of events as established in <u>Soviet history books</u>. Our view, however, is that Western researchers made a valuable contribution to the study of the period. Much of their work proved useful to <u>us, their Russian colleagues</u>, in the 1990s, when <u>we began</u> to <u>review</u> the <u>lessons of history</u> after <u>discarding</u> our ideological <u>blinkers</u>. This is why today <u>we so badly need</u> studies that would take into account the different interpretations of historical facts and events and <u>help</u> us make more objective, unbiased assessments, <u>not influenced by ideology</u>.

Появление новых <u>исследовательских трудов</u> по политической истории первых двух послевоенных десятилетий связано с дальнейшим расширением и <u>осмыслением источниковой базы</u>. В 90-е годы стали доступными многие <u>фонды архивных учреждений</u>, открылись <u>двери</u> партийных и государственных архивов. Поэтому последнее десятилетие <u>стало</u> прорывным в изучении советской истории. Данная работа, как и всякое историческое исследование, могла появиться, прежде всего, благодаря доступности комплекса источников.

New <u>research</u> on the political history of the first two postwar decades owes much to the greatly expanded range of <u>available sources</u> and <u>new interpretations</u> of the material. The 1990s opened up hitherto classified documents by unlocking Communist Party and Soviet government <u>archives</u>, and the last ten years have <u>witnessed</u> a real breakthrough in the study of Soviet history. The present work, like others in the field, appears today largely thanks to the historian's access to a new diversity of sources.

From a text on real estate –
plans for warehouse hubs in modern Russia:

<u>Ритейлеры, логисты и девелоперы</u>: кому нужнее склады в регионах?

<u>Retailers, logistics managers, developers—who has more of a need for warehouses in their regions</u>?

Несмотря на <u>доказанную мировой практикой перспективу</u> совмещения разных типов недвижимости (складской, офисной, торговой и развлекательной) <u>в рамках</u> <u>единого</u> комплекса, развитие складских проектов в России <u>упорно</u> поддерживает <u>чистоту жанра</u>. Крупных <u>транслогистических</u> центров здесь еще долгое время не будет.

Despite the favorable prospects for combining different forms of real estate (warehouse, office, sales and entertainment/recreational) in one property complex, as shown in practice around the world, development of warehouse projects in Russia is unwavering in its support of separate projects. It will be a long time before such large-scale centers come to this country.

До сих пор в регионах с энтузиазмом работали всего три компании, все три активно <u>пиарят</u> свои проекты, что, впрочем, <u>не влияет</u> на скорость строительства: девелопмент – бизнес <u>неторопливый</u>. В регионах <u>они сталкиваются</u> с <u>объективными</u> трудностями: отсутствием <u>подходящей для складского строительства</u> земли и <u>несговорчивостью</u> местных властей. Земля – это самая большая проблема для девелоперов, выходящих в регионы. <u>Крайне</u> трудно найти участок необходимого размера <u>в категории промышленного назначения</u>. Если промышленная земля <u>выгодно расположена относительно</u> транспортных магистралей, она очень дорогая.

Up until now only three companies put any real enthusiasm into work in the regions. All three are actively promoting their projects, though this has not had much effect on the speed of construction. Development is a slow business, what with the very real challenges associated with the lack of land suitable for warehouse construction and the additional difficulty of persuading local authorities. For developers heading out to the regions the biggest problem is land. It is very hard to find a parcel of land the right size that could be zoned for industrial purposes. If an industrial parcel is located near a main artery, it tends to be very expensive.

Сейчас компании ведут переговоры с руководством выбранных городов. Однако местные власти <u>будто бы сговорились</u> и поняли, что с девелоперами <u>можно торговаться</u>.

Currently, these companies are negotiating with the authorities of the cities being considered. But the local authorities seem to have gotten together and discovered that they too have bargaining power.

From an article about the Rostropovich memorial week in Washington DC:

В Вашингтоне в середине октября собирались <u>участники и гости</u> недели, посвященной памяти великого российского и американского музыканта, Маэстро Мстислава Ростроповича. Мы и не предполагали, что это время, осененное именем великого Человека, станет не только триумфом музыки, а и триумфом взаимного понимания и <u>духовного</u> единения. <u>Но</u> мало кто знал, что чуть ли не до последнего дня <u>этот праздник</u> был <u>на грани срыва</u>.

That October, young musicians and music-lovers of all ages were gathering in Washington to take part in a week-long tribute to a great Russian and American musician, Maestro Mstislav Rostropovich. We could not have known then that the week of celebrations, inspired by a great man, would turn out to be not only a triumph of music, but of mutual understanding and bonding as well. On another note, however, few of us were aware that plans for the entire week's events might soon be wrecked.

Идея собрать друзей и почитателей творчества Мстислава Леопольдовича принадлежит его старшей дочери Ольге, продолжающей одно из главных дел отца. Она руководит созданным им Фондом помощи молодым одаренным музыкантам. Решено было провести эту встречу в столице США <u>к 75-летию</u> вашингтонского Национального симфонического оркестра, главного, по словам самого Маэстро, его «музыкального ребенка». Растил и пестовал его Ростропович 17 лет и вывел в число самых достойных и известных в мире музыкальных коллективов.

The idea of bringing together friends and admirers of Rostropovich and his art belongs to his older daughter, Olga, who is carrying on one of her father's most important causes. She heads the foundation he set up to support gifted young musicians. It was decided to hold this event in the U.S. capital to mark the 75th anniversary of Washington's National Symphony Orchestra, which Rostropovich called his "premier musical child." For seventeen years the maestro worked with this orchestra, building it up and nurturing it until it was one of the best – and best-known – musical collectives in the world.

Сначала речь шла об одном концерте юных музыкантов – стипендиатов Фонда Ростроповича в <u>столичном Центре Искусств им.Кеннеди</u>, но оказалось, что у Славы (так просто и любовно Ростроповича зовут в Америке) столько друзей, такое множество поклонников его музыкального дара, что в программу включили еще несколько мероприятий. Все шло к тому, что в Вашингтоне состоится <u>грандиозный</u> музыкальный фестиваль. Имя Ростроповича открывало сердца и двери кабинетов высоких чиновников и бизнесменов.

At first the plans called for a single concert at the Kennedy Center for the Performing Arts featuring young musicians supported by the Rostropovich Foundation. But it turned out that Slava (the affectionate nickname by which America knew Rostropovich), had such legions of friends and admirers of his art that the program was enlarged to include several more important events. It looked as if the week would see a truly fabulous festival of music. Slava's name had opened many hearts, and also the doors to the offices of high-ranking officials in government, business, and the arts.

<u>И вот</u> - август 2008-го. <u>События</u> в Южной Осетии, обострение политических отношений в мире, а следом – финансовый кризис. Многие спонсоры ушли из проекта «<u>по-английски</u>» – тихо. Становилось очевидным, что «Посвящение Маэстро Ростроповичу» надо отменять. И только несколько человек не позволили сомнениям одолеть себя. Но нужно было чудо … и чудо свершилось.

But then came August 2008, and South Ossetia, ratcheting up political tensions in the world. After that, the financial crisis. Many of the sponsors of the event quietly faded away. It looked as if the week's tribute to the Maestro would have to be canceled. But a few courageous people refused to be daunted. What happened next was like a miracle.

День <u>приема</u> в российском посольстве был, пожалуй, самым волнующим для организаторов – были опасения, придут ли высокие американские гости в связи с нынешней политической ситуацией. <u>И вновь имя Ростроповича явило свою магическую силу, пришли все приглашенные</u>. Были приветственные речи, вспоминали талант и душу великого артиста.

The day the reception at the Russian Embassy was to take place was probably the most anxious for the organizers, who worried about the American officials invited to the event. With the political situation the way it was — would they come? But once again, Rostropovich's name worked its magic. Every one of the invitees did attend … There were speeches remembering the great artist's talent and his heart.

<u>А потом зазвучала Музыка</u>. Ольга Ростропович представляла исполнителей, которых Фонд помощи молодым талантам собирает по всей России.. <u>Приятным</u> сюрпризом стало выступление американских музыкантов из Национального симфонического оркестра, работавших с Ростроповичем. А когда хор Вашингтонского хорового общества исполнил на русском языке молитву Рахманинова, особенно любимую Ростроповичем, то подумалось, вот сейчас, в эту секунду, ничто не важно, ни национальность, ни профессия, ни богатство, ни общественное положение - <u>все вместе и одинаково</u> чувствуют <u>высокое</u> одухотворение. Пусть это и длится лишь несколько мгновений.

After the speeches came the music, and what music! Olga Rostropovich introduced the performers. The Foundation that supports gifted young musicians finds them all over Russia. A welcome surprise was the appearance of American musicians from the National Symphony Orchestra who had worked with Rostropovich. And when the Washington Choral Society performed a hymn by Rachmaninov in Russian, a work particularly beloved by Rostropovich, they were greeted with a standing ovation, many in the audience unable to hold back their tears. One thought was foremost: "Now, at this moment, nothing else matters, not your nationality, not your profession, nor how rich you are or what your social position might be – we all feel that this is a moment of inspiration, even if it only lasts a few moments."

На следующий день. на концерте молодых исполнителей в Центре им. Кеннеди зрителей и слушателей <u>ждали не менее глубокие впечатления</u>. … У <u>публики просто захватывало дух</u> от разнообразия дарований, от сочетания юности и зрелого мастерства. И снова зал аплодировал стоя. И тогда <u>Ольга Мстиславна,</u> заметно <u>волнуясь</u> поднялась на сцену, обняла своих подопечных и тихо произнесла в зал: «Спасибо вам всем. Я чувствую, что сейчас папа с нами».

The following day, the audience at the Kennedy Center heard more exciting performances. And once again the audience was on its feet, applauding the young artists for their talent, both diverse and mature. At that point, Olga stepped up on the stage. Embracing her young protégés and obviously emotional, she spoke to the audience in a low voice: "Thank you … thank you all. Right now, I feel that Papa is here … with us."

**From a text on orca whales off the Chukotka Peninsula
in the Russian Far East:**

Как хищник, стоящий на самой вершине пищевых цепей морских
экосистем косатки используют все доступные ресурсы, в том числе
и морских млекопитающих, включая крупных китов. Из литературы
известны многочисленные случаи нападения косаток на широкий
спектр видов морских млекопитающих. Из китообразных это
блювал Balaenoptera musculus и т.д.

A predator at the very top of the food chain in marine ecosystems, the
killer whale (*Orcinus orca*) utilizes every available food source, including
other marine mammals, even large whales. The literature cites numerous
cases of killer whale attacks on a wide range of marine mammal species.
Among the cetaceans are the blue whale *Balaenoptera musculus,...* etc.

Поиски потенциальных жертв косатки обычно ведут, патрулируя
прибрежные воды развернутым строем, фронтом или косой линией.
При охоте на серых китов выделяются несколько приемов. Охоту
начинают молодые животные и самки. Они стараются захватить
серого кита за хвостовую лопасть и грудные плавники. Всегда
стараются мешать дыханию кита наплывая на его дыхало, кусают в
область грудных ластов, рвут наиболее уязвимые подчелюстной
мешок и нижнюю челюсть (рис. 1).

Orcas usually search out potential prey by patrolling coastal waters
single file, over a wide front, or in diagonal formation. When hunting gray
whales, killer whales favor several tactics. Initiating the attack are
juveniles and adult females, which generally attempt to seize the gray
whale by its tail fluke and pectoral fins, thus tiring it and forcing it to stop.
They always try to impair the gray whale's breathing by swimming on top
of it, closing its blowhole, biting the whale in the area of its pectoral fins,
tearing at the vulnerable sub-mandibular sac and the jaw itself (Figure 1).

Этих приемов для молодых серых китов, по-видимому, <u>оказывается</u> <u>достаточно</u>. <u>Сильно травмированное, утомленное и ослабленное от</u> <u>потери крови животное погибает</u>. Такую охоту косаток на серого кита одному из авторов удалось наблюдать с <u>борта</u> <u>научно-исследо-</u> <u>вательского</u> судна «Академик Шулейкин» 27 июля 1997 г <u>в</u> <u>прибрежье</u> южной части Чукотского моря у поселка Уэлен. Место охоты хорошо было видно по всплескам, <u>фонтанам</u> и красному цвету воды. Когда судно подошло, судя по крови в воде, серый кит был уже ранен. В охоте принимала участие группа из 5 косаток – 3 крупных и 2 небольших. <u>Непосредственно</u> в нападениях участвовали одна крупная (судя по спинному плавнику самка) и небольшие косатки.

With young killer whales this routine is generally sufficient to kill the gray whale, badly injured, exhausted, and weak from loss of blood. On July 27, 1997, one of the authors of the present article witnessed such an attack by killer whales on a gray whale from the deck of the research vessel *Academician Shuleikin* in the coastal waters of the southern Chukchi Sea off Uelen village. The site was easy to identify because of the splashing, the numerous blows from their spouts/blow holes, and the reddened water. By the time the vessel approached the site, it was obvious that the whale had already been wounded. The hunt involved a pod of five killer whales—three large and two small. The actual attacks were carried out by one of the large whales (a female, judging from the dorsal fin) and the two smaller ones.

From "I was the Director of the Bolshoi":

… Прошло некоторое время. «Кармен-сюита» прочно утвердилась в репертуаре Большого театра. <u>Никаких дискриминационных мер</u> <u>Министерство культуры не предпринимало</u> и мы постепенно утвердились во мнении, что недавнее "обсуждение" <u>имело</u> <u>одноразовый, случайный характер</u>. Поэтому, когда балетная труппа театра стала готовиться в <u>очередную гастрольную поездку</u> – в этот раз в США – у руководства театра не было никаких оснований пересматривать гастрольный репертуар, согласованный <u>в свое время</u> с американской стороной и утвержденный тогда же Министерством культуры.

Time passed. *Carmen Suite* had found a secure place on the bills of the Bolshoi, and we all concluded that the recent "discussion" had been more or less a chance occurrence, with no further consequences. So when the ballet troupe began preparations for another foreign tour, this time to the U.S., we saw no reason to revise our repertory, which had months ago been agreed with the American side and confirmed by the Ministry of Culture of the USSR.

Как всегда в таких случаях, труппа вылетала в США на самолете, а крупногабаритные декорации и костюмы, упакованные в больших контейнерах, пересылались морем и следовательно, нужно было предусмотреть в графике перевозок не менее 25-30 дней, которые потребуются, чтобы груз был упакован, переслан в Ленинград, перетранспортирован на рейсовое океанское судно, выгружен в порту назначения и доставлен к месту первого выступления.

As always in such cases, the company was flying, while all bulky scenery and costumes would go by boat, so that we had to allow 25 to 30 days extra to pack the cargo, ship it to Leningrad, load it onto an ocean-going steamer, unload it in the port of destination, and deliver it to the site of our first performance in the U.S.

И вот именно в этот самый период, когда балетная труппа еще давала последние представления на сцене Большого театра, а декорационное имущество гастрольных спектаклей уже было отправлено в далекий путь к заокеанским берегам, мне позвонила Е.А. Фурцева и в повышенном тоне стала чинить допрос по поводу начинающиеся через две недели выступлений Большого балета в Америке. Я ответил, что план поездки был более полугода назад согласован с американской стороной, ...что принятые договорные обязательства всегда разрабатывались с участием ответственных сотрудников Министерства культуры СССР и утверждались его руководством.

Most of this had already been done, and the company was giving its final performances in Moscow before leaving on tour when suddenly – a phone call from the Ministry. An agitated Furtseva demanded a full report on what the Bolshoi Ballet was going to be showing in the U.S. – and the tour was only two weeks away! I replied as calmly as I could that the plans had been agreed more than six months before, that in normal business relations with organizations in other countries, there was no room for arbitrary action, one-sided decisions, or any violation of commitments, particularly since these were always worked out with Culture Mininistry officials and signed by the Minister herself.

Для меня стало ясно, что нервозное состояние Фурцевой объяснялось тем, что ее, видимо, спросили, на каком основании в гастроли по США назначена «Кармен-сюита», а она, по своему обыкновению, свалила все на своеволие руководства театра. И уж тут никакие объяснения … все мои доводы не были приняты во внимание раздраженной министершей.

Furtseva's attack of nerves was clearly the result of her having been "asked" (the term she used when anything in her jurisdiction was causing displeasure at the top. She would then be "asked," and we were likely to hear her snap: "It's easy for you to talk. I may well be asked ...!") Our Minister had apparently been challenged to explain on what grounds Carmen Suite was to be performed in the U.S., of all places. And she, as was her wont, blamed everything on the obstreperous director of the Bolshoi. And nothing I could say about that could make the wrathful lady listen to reason.

Она потребовала не отправлять декорации «Кармен-сюиты» в Ленинград! Я ответил, что они уже отправлены. Тогда она велела не грузить их на судно! Я ответил, что они уже давно погружены. Тут она распорядилась немедленно сгрузить их с судна на причал! Я сообщил, что судно уже вышло в море. Тогда она сказала, чтобы судно немедленно задержали в открытом море и перегрузили декорации на какое-нибудь местное плавучее средство (на буксир?) для переброски обратно в порт! Очевидно, ей не терпелось срочно доложить «наверх» о принятии всех мер к недопущению неблагонадежной «Кармен-сюиты» к гастролям в Америке.

She demanded that the sets for *Carmen Suite* remain in Moscow and not be sent to Leningrad.
"They've already been sent."
She ordered them held up in port and not loaded with everything else.
"The ship is on the high seas."
"Have it stopped then! Let the sets be unloaded onto a local vessel (a tug?) and taken back to Leningrad!"
What she obviously needed – right away – was to be able to report "upstairs" that all effective measures had been taken to prevent the troublesome ballet from being shown in America.

Когда я как можно тверже сказал, что предлагаемая ею операция абсолютно нереальна, она еще долго бушевала и <u>относительно</u> <u>успокоилась лишь после того</u>, как я заверил, что декорации не будут выгружены в порту назначения, а будут отсортированы и оставлены в трюме судна, с которым и возвратятся неиспользованными в СССР.

I said in the firmest voice I could muster that any such operation was totally unrealistic, but the storm continued unabated. Finally, I had to assure her that yes, the *Carmen* sets would stay in the port of destination, yes, they would be separated from the rest, and yes, they would remain on board, returning unused to the Soviet Union when the ship sailed home.

Сейчас покажется невероятным, что такой популярный балет, <u>вошедший в репертуар</u> многих театров мира, мог показаться кое-кому крамольным. Но ведь еще <u>здравствуют и имеют</u> <u>прикосновение к искусству</u> те, кому еще двадцать лет назад «Кармен-сюита» казалась проявлением формализма, и <u>нет никаких</u> <u>гарантий</u>, что <u>их вкусы сколько-нибудь изменились</u> за этот период времени.

Today it is hard to believe that such a popular ballet, staged by companies around the world, could ever have struck anyone as a call to high treason. Yet some of those who twenty years ago found *Carmen Suite* the worst kind of "formalism" may still retain control over artistic affairs. Their tastes have not changed, and neither, I expect, have their spots.

Glossary

"All-purpose" verb: a verb vague in meaning without a key word accompanying it, that is often overused in Russian (e.g., осуществлять *"carry out"* or *"implement"*)

Augmentative: in Russian, having the property of increasing, in actual size or emotionally, and reinforcing the idea of the original word

Body language: used figuratively, often an Anglo-Saxon verb characterizing an action attributable to a living being

Calque: a loan word from another langauge, usually a literal translation; for example, the English word *"skyscraper"* turns into "небоскрёб"

Cognate: a look-alike that often suggests itself as a "natural" equivalent in translation

Diminutive: implies smallness, either actual or imputed in token of affection, scorn, or other emotion

Identifier: a label or category supplied to aid comprehension

Modals: the grammatical forms (e.g., *should, would, may, might,* etc) that actually alter the meaning of a verb

"Modals": words or phrases that would seem to tone down the original Russian, but often rhetorically serve to emphasize the thought

Pragmatic factors: words added to a translation to clarify a thought or bring it in line with the original

Process noun: in Russian, a noun derived from a verb with an ending such as -ание, etc., as in признание from признавать, but also including those with the same root as the verb, as in сушка from сушить

Prop: an accessory supporting the key word or words, whether required grammatically or used for balance

Register: the style level of the text, such as formal, colloquial, etc.

Rhetorical factors: words, other than the literal translation, employed to produce the same emotional effect in translation as they do in the original

Semantic: relating to meaning, including denotation and/or connotation

Source language: the words of the <u>original</u> text; for example, in Russian-English translation, the source language is Russian

Target language: the words of the <u>translated</u> text; for example, in Russian-English translation, the target language is English

Bibliography

Glenn, E.S. "Semantic Difficulties in International Communication." *The Use and Misuse of Language*. Ed. S.I. Hayakawa. Greenwich, Connecticut: Fawcett Publications, 1962, pp. 47-69.

Krylova, O., and Khavronina, S. *Word Order in Russian Sentences*. Moscow: Russian Language Publishers, 1976. 2nd ed., rev. Moscow: Russky Yazyk, 1988.

Lubensky, Sophia. *Russian-English Dictionary of Idioms*. New York: Random House, 1995.

Marder, Stephen. *A Supplementary Russian-English Dictionary*. Columbus, Ohio: Slavica Publishers, 1992.

Visson, Lynn. *From Russian Into English: An Introduction to Simultaneous Interpretation*. 2nd edition. Newburyport, MA: Focus Publishing, R. Pullins and Company, 1999.

Стрелкова, Н.С. *Ключи для пособия по практической стилистике английского языка и стилистическому редактированию переводов*. Москва: МГПИИЯ, 1980.

Стрелкова, Н.С. *Практическая стилистика английского языка и стилистическое редактирование переводов* ч.3 Москва: МГПИИЯ, 1982.

Стрелкова, Н.С. *Учебное пособие по практической стилистике английского языка и стилистическому редактированию переводов* Москва: МГПИИЯ, 1984.

Виссон, Линн. *Русские проблемы в английской речи: слова и фразы мы в контексте двух культур*. Москва: Р.Валент, 1997.

П. Р. Палажченко. *Мой несистематический словарь: русско-английский/ англо-русский, I и II*. Москва: Р.Валент, 2009.

About the Author

In my own experience, early exposure to translation techniques while in the U.S. might have saved me time and been a lot of fun besides, but I mostly learned the long, if not the hard way, by doing. True, it was "with a little help from my friends" – my colleagues, the translators' community, and of course, books. Russian was the main language in our family, making me a "native" speaker of Russian – also called a heritage speaker. Yet since children learn quickly, English soon joined Russian, often with both languages in the same sentence. A decade later high school introduced me to French and Latin; more French at college gave me a little experience in translation. After graduation, and two more years teaching these same subjects at high schools in New England, the Russian heritage part of my makeup prompted me to take advantage of the Khrushchev "thaw" to travel to the Soviet Union. Once in Moscow, I was immediately asked to fill a job vacancy at Radio Moscow as a translation "style editor" (the equivalent of a copy editor in the United States). Within a few months a young Russian reporter (with excellent BBC English, by the way) became my husband. And so I stayed on— for 35 years.

At first, that editing job, and occasional translation assignments, depended heavily on intuition, though with constant reference to the one Russian-English dictionary in the department. Not having had any formal training in Russian, only vaguely sensed how different it was from English in things like word order, personal-impersonal, and active-passive relationships, the various ways of emphasizing a point, and appropriate register. It was my job, I thought, to winnow out the bare meaning of the original. When intuition did not help, never having been shown the tricks of the trade, I was sometimes forced to go word-for-word with only minor adjustments to prevent a translation from sounding too foreign. Gradually, I began to see through the surface forms and rhetoric to the deeper structure and the intention of the author, but it was not until years later, when I started teaching translation of Russian into English at what was then Moscow's Maurice Thorez Institute of Foreign Languages, that a system slowly formed in my mind. I had the sole responsibility—and the excitement—of helping my students advance their skills writing and translating into English. During the last 20 years of a 24-year tenure at this post-graduate translation course my students were mostly professionals, with very advanced English and an extensive cultural background. Employed as translators, editors, and English teachers, they had a

aturity and a motivation that compelled them to study ever harder, with unfail-
g enthusiasm, in spite of a part-time work load at their day jobs for some of
em.

Officially, my job at the Institute was to provide Practice in the English Lan-
iage and Stylistic Editing of Translations. In fact, both the "practice" and the
diting" were based on translation itself, with techniques discovered in the
ocess. We all hoped the enthusiasm generated by those little epiphanies would
main with the students throughout their careers. What I gained from those years
experience provided precious material for my own use and, I hope, for future
nerations of translators.

After my return to the United States in 1992, I continued to teach, briefly as
a adjunct at Georgetown University and American University, and to translate
r the National Park Service and the TV program *Frontline*, with a dozen as-
gnments in court interpreting, and, longest of all, an eight-year stint on the
eringia Project (reports and conferences in Anchorage and Barrow, Alaska).
hroughout this time, a plan slowly crystallized in my mind – to write the book
ou now hold in your hands. In it I have tried to put to good use my teaching and
anslation experience, passing on the skills and techniques I discovered over the
ears. It's been an exciting time and I am ready for more. I am now working on
a interactive online course for translators.

New Beginner's Guides with Interactive Online Workbook

Hippocrene Beginner's Guides are available in over 40 languages, an now in an innovative new format! Instead of audio CDs, students will hav access to an interactive companion website with video, audio, and sel correcting exercises that provide quality, hands-on experience with th language. The books contain the carefully-paced and relevant lessons th Hippocrene Beginners Guides are known for, with dialogues on everyda topics such as eating out and sightseeing, grammar explained in accessibl steps, and exercises throughout.

Ideal for both classroom use and self-study, Beginner's Guides with Ir teractive Online Workbook are now available for Russian and Ukrainiar written by highly regarded and experienced professors.

BEGINNER'S UKRAINIAN WITH INTERACTIVE ONLINE WORKBOOK
Yuri Shevchuk
Published 8/2011 • ISBN 978-0-7818-1268-9 • $35.00 pb

BEGINNER'S RUSSIAN WITH INTERACTIVE ONLINE WORKBOOK
Anna S. Kudyma, Frank J. Miller, and Olga E. Kagan
Published 7/2010 • ISBN 978-0-7818-1251-1 • $35.00 pb

Other Russian Titles from Hippocrene

Russian-English/English-Russian Dictionary & Phrasebook
4,000 entries · ISBN 978-0-7818-1003-6 · $14.95 pb

Russian-English/English-Russian Concise Dictionary
10,000 entries · ISBN 978-0-7818-0132-4· $12.95 pb

Russian-English/English-Russian Practical Dictionary
35,000 entries · ISBN 978-0-7818-1243-6· $24.95 pb

Russian-English/English-Russian Standard Dictionary
With Complete Phonetics
32,000 entries · ISBN 978-0-7818-0280-2· $19.95 pb

Russian-English/English-Russian Pocket Legal Dictionary
6,000 entries · ISBN 978-0-7818-1222-1 · $19.95 pb

The Comparative Russian-English Dictionary of Russian Proverbs and Sayings
5,343 entries · ISBN 978-0-7818-0424-0· $35.00 pb

Hippocrene Children's Illustrated Russian Dictionary
500 entries · ISBN 978-0-7818-0892-7 · $14.95 pb

English-Russian Comprehensive Dictionary
50,000 entries · ISBN 978-0-7818-0506-3· $35.00 pb

Russian-English Comprehensive Dictionary
40,000 entries · ISBN 978-0-7818-0506-3· $60.00 hc

Also available from Hippocrene Books

Byelorussian-English/English-Byelorussian Concise Dictionary
10,000 entries · ISBN 978-0-8705-2114-0· $9.95 pb

Chechen-English/English-Chechen Dictionary & Phrasebook
1,400 entries · ISBN 978-0-7818-0446-2· $11.95 pb

Beginner's Croatian with 2 Audio CDs
ISBN 978-0-7818-1232-0 · $29.95 pb

Croatian-English/English-Croatian Dictionary & Phrasebook
4,500 entries · ISBN 978-0-7818-0810-1· $11.95 pb

Estonian-English/English-Estonian Dictionary & Phrasebook
3,700 entries · ISBN 978-0-7818-0931-3· $11.95 pb

Estonian-English/English-Estonian Concise Dictionary
6,500 entries · ISBN 978-0-7818-0931-3· $11.95 pb

Beginner's Georgian with 2 Audio CDs
ISBN 978-0-7818-1230-6 · $29.95 pb

Beginner's Hungarian with 2 Audio CDs
ISBN 978-0-7818-1192-7 · S26.95 pb

Latvian-English/English-Latvian Dictionary & Phrasebook
3,000 entries · ISBN 978-0-7818-1008-1· $13.95 pb

Latvian-English/English-Latvian Practical Dictionary
16,000 entries · ISBN 978-0-7818-0059-4·$16.95 pb

Lithuanian-English/English-Lithuanian Concise Dictionary
8,000 entries · ISBN 978-0-7818-0151-5· $14.95 pb

Lithuanian-English/English-Lithuanian Dictionary & Phrasebook
4,500 entries · ISBN 978-0-7818-1009-8 · $14.95 pb

Beginner's Polish
ISBN 978-0-7818-0299-4· $9.95 pb

Mastering Polish with 2 Audio CDs
ISBN 978-0-7818-1065-4· $29.95 pb

Polish-English/English-Polish Dictionary (American English Edition)
30,000 entries · ISBN 978-0-7818-1237-5 · $ 22.95 pb

Polish-English/English-Polish Concise Dictionary *With Complete Phonetics*
8,000 entries · ISBN 978-0-7818-0133-1· $12.95 pb

Romanian-English/English-Romanian Dictionary & Phrasebook
5,500 entries · ISBN 978-0-7818-0921-4· $ 12.95 pb

Romanian-English/English-Romanian Practical Dictionary
20,000 entries · ISBN 978-0-7818-1224-5 · $24.95 pb

Beginner's Serbo-Croatian
ISBN 978-0-7818-0845-3· $14.95 pb

Slovak-English/English-Slovak Concise Dictionary
7,500 entries · ISBN 978-0-8705-2115-7· $14.95 pb

Slovene-English/English-Slovene Dictionary & Phrasebook
3,500 entries · ISBN 978-0-7818-1047-0· $14.95 pb

Ukrainian-English/English-Ukrainian Practical Dictionary
Revised Edition with Menu Terms
8,000 entries · ISBN 978-0-7818-0306-9· $19.95 pb

Ukrainian Phrasebook and Dictionary
3,000 entries · ISBN 978-0-7818-0188-1· $12.95 pb

Prices subject to change without prior notice. **To purchase Hippocrene Books** contact your local bookstore, visit www.hippocrenebooks.com, call (212) 685-4373, or write to: HIPPOCRENE BOOKS, 171 Madison Avenue, New York, NY 10016.

www.ingramcontent.com/pod-product-compliance
Lightning Source LLC
Jackson TN
JSHW011402130125
77033JS00023B/801